VISION OF FATIMA

FR. THOMAS MCGLYNN, O.P.

VISION *of* FATIMA

SOPHIA INSTITUTE PRESS
Manchester, New Hampshire

Vision of Fatima was originally published by Little, Brown and Company, Boston, in 1948.

In accordance with the decrees of Urban VIII, the author declares that his opinions on all matters treated in this book are entirely subject to the judgment of the Holy See.

Cover design by Perceptions Design Studio.

On the cover: Our Lady of Fatima Church, Hartford, Connecticut,
Copyright © 2010 Bob Mullen, The Catholic Photographer.

Scripture passages in this book are taken from the Douay-Rheims Version of the Bible.

Revisores: Thomas F. Carey, O.P., Ph.D.; Thomas Shanley, O.P., A.B.

Imprimi Potest: Terentius Stephanus
McDermott, O.P., S.T.L., LL.D., *Prior Provincialis*

Nihil obstat: Right Reverend Hugh F. Blunt, LL.D., *Censor Librorum*

Imprimatur: +Most Reverend Richard J. Cushing, D.D., Archbishop of Boston

Sophia Institute Press
Box 5284, Manchester, NH 03108
1-800-888-9344

www.SophiaInstitute.com

Library of Congress Cataloging-in-Publication Data
To come

First printing

CONTENTS

VISION OF FATIMA

1

BEGINNINGS

The statue, in its new plywood case, rested on a seat during the takeoff. Soon the lights of New York were lost in the overcast, and the hurry of preparation was happily left below. I could relax.

Only a few weeks had passed since I had made up my mind to see Lucy. The directors of the company for which I was to make a statue of Our Lady of Fatima were satisfied with the little model. They would accept an enlargement as the first in a series of statues I had agreed to design. I wanted to be more certain, however. Although I believed that the model conformed with the description of the vision credited to Lucy, I thought it best to seek her approval or criticism of the treatment and symbolism that I had worked out.

When the plane attained cruising altitude and we could move about, I found, with the help of the stewardess and purser, a convenient rod in the baggage section of the cabin to which the box could be strapped and made secure against jarring.

VISION OF FATIMA

The box looked so much like a carpenter's toolkit, and I looked so little like a carpenter that questions were soon asked. Over coffee in the galley of the plane, at breakfast in the airport at Gander, Newfoundland, and in the cabin during the long, bright flight over the Atlantic, I had to tell many times of the contents of the box, the reason for my trip, and the story of Fatima.

I was on my way to Portugal in hopes of visiting a nun who, as a child, was one of three to whom the Blessed Virgin appeared in 1917 near a village called Fatima. If permitted to see her, I would show her this statue as the means of obtaining from her a complete description of the apparition.

The story began for the world when, on the evening of May 13, 1917, a lively little girl of seven who lived in the village of Aljustrel in Portugal said to her mother: "Mother, we saw the Blessed Virgin today at the Cova!"

The world, in the person of Jacinta's mother, Olimpia Marto, was incredulous, at first. But she was puzzled when Jacinta's brother of nine, Francis, simply confirmed the claim.

When the story spread through the village, it encountered hostile unbelief, especially at the home of Lucy, the ten-year-old leader of the group and cousin of the other two. Lucy's severely upright mother, Maria Rosa dos Santos, beat her for having told a shameful lie.

Lucy had to recount the happening to the parish priest.

The three had been playing at the top of a hollow in a field, known as the Cova da Iria, about a mile and a half from home. A flash of lightning in a cloudless sky had startled them and prompted them to herd the sheep hastily down the hill toward Aljustrel. When they had reached the bottom, another flash had stopped them.

A beautiful young lady, clothed in brilliant white light, had appeared before them, standing on top of a small holm oak tree, her hands joined in prayer. She had calmed their fears.

Conversation had followed between the Lady and Lucy in which the children had been instructed to pray the Rosary and to return to the same place on the thirteenth day of each month until October. She had promised that in October she would tell them who she was and what she desired.

The apparition had lasted about ten minutes. Then the Lady, without moving her feet, had left the tree, gone toward the east, and disappeared in the distance.

The priest was not convinced of the supernatural character of the incident that was related, but he was aware of Lucy's simplicity. Perhaps the devil, or hallucination, but hardly deceit. He advised Maria Rosa to let Lucy return to the Cova in June but instructed that Lucy should be brought back again if anything further should be reported.

Everyone from Aljustrel avoided the Cova on June 13 in angry contempt of the children's claim. But a handful of people gathered from other villages.

Afterward some of these declared their observation of strange phenomena during the period of the apparition. Some said the light of the sun was dimmed; others, that the tree bent down as if under a weight; others, that the leaves of the tree turned eastward when the children made known the departure of the Lady.

These reports spread throughout the mountain region rapidly. As a result very large crowds were present at all the following apparitions.

Study of the new incidents convinced the priest that the devil was at work. His opinion frightened Lucy. Not until July

13, shortly before the time appointed for the apparition, did she overcome her fears. A strong impulse changed her decision to stay away from the Cova, and she joined the others.

Because of all this mental torment Lucy asked the Lady, in July, to perform a miracle so that all would be convinced of the truth of the apparitions.

At the conclusion of this visit the crowd was informed of two things: that the Lady had told the children a "Secret"; and that she had promised to work a miracle in October.

On August 13 the anticlerical administrator of the district kidnapped the children and took them to the town of Vila Nova d'Ourem. He tried to get the Secret from them, first by pleading, then by threatening, then by pretending to fulfill his threats. He put them in a cell with common criminals. Later, after a final demand for the revelation of the Secret, he enacted the procedure of condemning them, one at a time, to death in boiling oil. Each in turn stood firm, accepted the sentence, and prepared for death.

Meantime, the thousands who were at the Cova on August 13 in the children's absence bore witness to an explosive noise near the tree, to rainbow lights playing on the ground, and to what appeared to be flowers falling from the sky.

On August 19, after the defeated administrator had brought them back to Fatima, the children reported the fourth visit of the Lady as having taken place in another field, called Valinhos.

Many who attended in September saw a luminous globe hover over the tree during the time that the children were in ecstasy.

The general estimate of the crowd present at the Cova on October 13 is seventy thousand. The great attraction was the miracle that Lucy had promised. The devout came, bent on seeing it; scoffers in numbers came to see the devout disappointed.

People of all professions and classes were there, including reporters and photographers from Lisbon newspapers.

It had been raining torrentially all morning. At Lucy's words, "Look at the sun!" the rain stopped suddenly, the clouds above split apart, and, for most, the sun was visible in a blue sky. It could be looked upon without causing eyestrain. It seemed to spin on its axis. As it did, the clouds, people, trees, and other objects on the earth changed colors, becoming successively all blue, all yellow, all red, and so on. Then the sun seemed to descend toward the earth.

The crowd's first reaction of wonder changed to terror with the apparent fall of the sun. People went down on their knees and made desperate acts of faith and contrition.

Suddenly the downward course of the sun stopped, and it resumed its normal position and blinding, noonday brilliance.

After the miracle, a man lifted Lucy up and asked her to tell the crowd what the Lady had said.

Lucy said that the Lady had identified herself as "the Lady of the Rosary"; that she had warned men to amend their lives, in the words: "Do not offend our Lord any more. He is already much offended"; that she had promised an early ending of the war; that she had asked people to pray the Rosary; and that she had requested that a chapel be built there in her honor.

Fatima, or, more properly, the Cova da Iria near Fatima, has attracted the devotion of the faithful in the form of great pilgrimages from that day. A small chapel was built in 1919 at the place where the tree had been. (The devout had removed the branches of the tree for precious relics even before the last apparition.) This chapel was dynamited by anticlericals in 1922. Soon afterward another was built in its place.

Church authorities delayed recognition of the apparitions for a long time. A bishop was appointed to the See of Leiria, in which Fatima lies, in 1920. In 1922 he selected a commission of theologians and instituted the process of investigation. The study took seven years. A year after its completion the bishop declared in a 1930 pastoral letter the credibility of the apparitions.

Miraculous cures and remarkable conversions have been numerous at Fatima from the beginning.

A large basilica, the largest church in Portugal, is now nearing completion at the north end and on the highest spot of the Cova. On the west side are a retreat house and a hospital; another hospital is under construction on the east side. A large fountain occupies the center of the Cova. A little to the west, at the spot where the apparitions took place, is the Chapel of the Apparitions.

Francis and Jacinta Marto knew from the apparitions, and let it be known, that they were soon going to die. Both contracted influenza in 1918. Francis died in 1919; Jacinta, in 1920. Both had attained extraordinary spiritual maturity. They willingly offered their suffering and death to make reparation for sin.

Four years after the apparitions the bishop recommended to Lucy's parents that she be placed in an orphanage. The parents and Lucy gladly agreed. The plan would spare them the trials of innumerable visitors and endless interrogations. Lucy went to a school in the north of Portugal. Her name was changed to Maria das Dores so that her connection with Fatima would be unknown to her companions. In 1925 she was admitted to the Novitiate of the Sisters of Saint Dorothy in Tui, Spain. She remained there until 1946, when her superiors brought her back to Portugal.

Until 1942, this was substantially all that the world knew of the story and meaning of the Fatima apparitions.

Passengers and crew members who heard the story on that day over the Atlantic all heard it for the first time and with noticeable surprise.

"And Lucy is still living!" some would remark. "How old is she?"

"Forty."

Sufficient data had been given for easy computation of her age, but it seemed incredible that anyone still living could have had part in the miraculous, which is usually so remote that it can be affirmed or denied without difficulty. No demand was made upon the faith of those who heard the story. Thus far it was in every detail a matter of fairly recent and fully evident fact.

Acceptance of the full meaning and message of Fatima, however, as it has recently become known, does require trust in the honesty of Lucy and in the clear-sightedness of the ecclesiastical authority that now confirms her testimony.

On the silver jubilee of the apparitions in 1942 the Church released information on Fatima that elaborated and magnified its meaning. Part of this information was given by Lucy in 1927; most of the remainder is based on writings that she began in obedience to the bishop in 1935.

For the first time, and with Lucy now the sole witness, the public learned that an angel had appeared three times to the children in 1916. The dialogue, at least partial, of the apparitions was detailed; it brought out our Lady's pleas to the children that they make sacrifices for sinners. The intimate story of the children's life of habitual prayer and self-denial was published. The revelation of the Immaculate Heart of Mary during the June apparition came to light. But the disclosure that did most to create the current interest in Fatima was the unveiling of parts of the Secret confided to the children in July 1917.

The first part of the Secret was a vision of hell; the second part was the manifestation of God's will that devotion to the Immaculate Heart be established in the world.

A third part remains known only to Lucy. It is reported to have been written out by her and to be in the possession of the bishop of Leiria in an envelope bearing her instruction that it should not be opened until 1960.[1]

Coupled with many recorded statements of the Blessed Virgin during the apparitions, the vision of hell points up the terrifying fact of damnation and the probability that it claims a great many souls.

Devotion to the Immaculate Heart is presented in the second part of the Secret as the special help designated by God for man to escape hell. This devotion is given further emphasis by being made a necessary means of rescue from temporal disaster. In this second part of the Secret, the Blessed Virgin predicted the ending of the First World War and the beginning of the Second. She foretold also the spread of Russia's errors through the world with resultant wars, persecution of the Church, and the destruction of many nations.

[1] For more information on the Secret, see Tarcisio Bertone, S.D.B., "The Message of Fatima," Vatican website, http://www.vatican.va/roman_curia/congregations/cfaith/documents/rc_con_cfaith_doc_20000626_message-fatima_en.html. —Ed.

She said, further, in 1917 that she would come back to ask for Communions of reparation and for the consecration of Russia to her Immaculate Heart. Finally, she declared that Russia would be converted through her Immaculate Heart and that the world would be given a period of peace.

According to the disclosures of 1942, the Blessed Virgin has appeared several times since 1917 to Lucy. The first reported fulfillment of her promise to return occurred in 1925. She then made known to Lucy the devotion of the Communions of reparation of the Five First Saturdays. The faithful were promised assistance at the hour of death with the graces necessary for salvation in reward for receiving the sacraments of Confession and Communion, praying the Rosary, and meditating for fifteen minutes on the mysteries of the Rosary on the first Saturday of each of five consecutive months.

She communicated her wish that the Holy Father, joined by the bishops of the world on the same day, consecrate Russia to her Immaculate Heart.

The early history of Fatima had been familiar to me for several years. It presented no difficulty; it was another of the many credible apparitions of the Blessed Virgin. Neither did it arouse action. But the new information demanded action. If the message of Fatima as now understood is true, the fate of mankind in time and eternity is affected by it. The Church had certainly given every phase of Lucy's communications ample study before releasing these further data on Fatima.

It was a pity that everyone did not know about Fatima. Priests must make Fatima known. This, my companions in the clouds learned, was the reason why a priest was flying to Portugal with such an odd-looking piece of luggage.

As the prospect of seeing Lucy came closer, the statue was all but forgotten. Fatima, only a little while ago so far away, was in the country just ahead.

It was after midnight on February 1, 1947. The lights of Lisbon broke out of the night. They made a wavy pattern over the hills. "The lamp of our Lady," as Jacinta loved to call the moon, was shining on the harbor.

2

LISBON

"Ah! *Nossa Senhora de Fátima!*"

The customs officer was the first Portuguese person I met in Portugal. It was good to see and hear his pleasure in the discovery that my statue was an image of Our Lady of Fatima. It was also convenient, because he passed the rest of my luggage without inspection.

The plan of procedure had been well rehearsed. It was now too late to go to the Dominicans in Lisbon—although I was sure they were expecting me, for I had cabled from New York—but I would say Mass there in the morning. One of them would bring me to meet Cardinal Cerejeira. I would present the introduction that Cardinal Spellman had provided. The cardinal would then give me a letter of introduction to the bishop of Leiria. I would go there without delay, perhaps that very day, obtain the bishop's permission to see Lucy, and then, after a short stop at Fatima, proceed to the north for the visit.

Lucy might suggest a few alterations in details of the statue, but I had little doubt of its meeting with her general approval.

If she made corrections I would put them in drawings, and, if permitted a second visit, I would show the renditions to her for final verification. Between the statue and the drawings I would then have the whole, accurate picture of the vision of Our Lady of Fatima.

Fortified with Lucy's absolute or modified approval of the design, I would then go to Rome and ask the Holy Father's blessing on the statue.

Now that I was through customs, I was impatient to get on to Lisbon. It was a shock to find out that I wasn't going to Lisbon after all but to Estoril, wherever that was. The airline agent was very sorry, but there was no hotel space available in Lisbon that night.

So, to Estoril. The taxi driver gripped the wheel, sat on the edge of the seat, and we were off! Before he had the old but eager engine in high gear, I noticed the pleasant expanse of parkway, bordered with lines of young eucalyptus trees, through which we drove away from the airport.

With the urgency and speed of an ambulance chase, we were soon bounding over the broad avenues of Lisbon, protected at crossings only by the excited blare of our shrill horn. The glimpses of Lisbon on that night ride gave an impression of its antiquity and charm. The boulevards were spacious and well landscaped. There was harmony of design in the ceramic-trimmed buildings with high, flat façades, crossed at different levels by finely wrought iron balconies. Sidewalks were made of black and white rock, set in mosaic-like patterns. Quaint, narrow streets curved upward from the Avenidas to Lisbon's many hills.

The way out of Lisbon to Monte Estoril was along Portugal's renowned Riviera. Villas, monasteries, forts, and palaces stood out in bluish silhouette, surrounded by the rich foliage of palm, acacia, and olive trees that glistened as though lacquered with silver in the moonlight. A cool breeze was blowing off the waters of the Tagus estuary.

Within an hour we ascended the imposing, cliff-like town of Estoril and stopped in a narrow square before an eighteenth-century hotel. An attractive, modern interior was small compensation for the chill of my room. Nor did the historical experience of being in a place famed for its loveliness among Phoenicians, Greeks, and Romans make up for the delay of my plans.

In the morning I went to the little baroque church of Santo Antonio, which was situated serenely in an environment of palatial dwellings with luxuriant gardens, on a wide, steeply curving road that overlooked the sea.

It was the first Saturday of February. The filled church was evidence of response to the Fatima appeal for Communions of reparation on the First Saturdays.

My altar boy waited in a sleeveless red cassock, which was more a formality than a garment. An open door admitted the chill morning air across a slate floor to the timeworn vestment case, where I prepared for Mass.

On passing by the sanctuary I noticed that the main altar all but filled the wall space up to the ceiling with its heavily ornate forms. There was a statue of Saint Dominic on the Gospel side of the altar. The Rosary, which he had introduced to the world, was being droned out in rhythmic cadences by the congregation.

After Mass I had a brief visit with three Italian priests of the Salesian Order, in a school adjoining the church. They were very proud that a nephew of Jacinta (the youngest of the three children of Fatima) was a member of their order. They gave me a book on Fatima that another Salesian had written. He, too, they said, had visited Lucy. How very fortunate I was, they thought, to be on my way to see her. I shared the thought, but I had reluctantly to note that my visit was not at all assured as yet.

I went back to Lisbon by an electric railway. The new and clean-looking station fitted well the rich beauty of Estoril's bright homes. The train was powered by an overhead trolley. It was very neat and modern-looking.

The passengers, handsome and well-dressed, were, I supposed, mostly on shopping missions, but, although they were probably as serious as any suburban commuters, the sunlight that filled the car made them appear quite pleased with the trip.

A little girl who sat facing me in a seat ahead appealed to me as a fine subject for a sketch. I thought she was about the age that Lucy was at the time of the apparitions. She was much prettier than photographs show Lucy to have been, but I imagined that she had similar racial features—large, dark eyes and firm, full cheeks. She was all dressed up in brown and pink and seemed to be making a splendid effort not to show how much fun she thought it was to be going with mother to "Lisboa."

At times when I put down the pad to conceal my drawing activity, I saw beautiful farmlands, estates, and gardens rolling past the window. This unplanned detour to Estoril provided some of the most colorful landscapes to be seen in Portugal.

The terminal in Lisbon was at the Cais do Sodré, a wide, sloping plaza at the waterfront from which busy, narrow streets run east and west, crowded with markets and small shops, at the foot of the city's central hill. The square was an expanse of cobblestones, empty in the center except for a line of small taxicabs; but at its edges the bustle of the city began. Cars, with their horns incessantly piping, were darting in every direction at the heels of unheeding pedestrians, women with heavy burdens on their heads, laborers, shop and office workers, merchants.

I showed the address of the Dominicans to a taxi driver. Two boys in ragged suits, offering their services, pleaded hopelessly with me. I gathered later that they must have been telling me that they could easily carry the bags to the address, because, after I squeezed myself and the three pieces of luggage into the tiny seat of the taxi, I hardly had time to settle down before the driver went a short block beyond the square, turned into a little street and stopped in front of the large, double door of a flat, grayish building. It was the monastery of Corpo Santo.

The sidewalk was wide enough for only one person. When a diminutive streetcar, jammed with passengers, swung around on the narrow-gauge tracks, it came menacingly close to me as I waited.

The door, set in a massive wall, opened directly to a steep staircase. At its top the porter, a young Portuguese who had pulled the cord to release the door bolt, waited inquiringly. The only explanation I could give him was the clumsy operation of getting the case and two bags inside the door.

My cable had not arrived. I was disappointed to have broken in on the community unannounced. But notice was not necessary, for a most cordial reception and fraternal interest in my mission on the part of Father Enda McVeigh, the superior, and all the fathers and brothers of the monastery.

Apart from the handsome appointments provided for visitors in the parlor, the furnishings of the house showed signs of age and poverty. The rambling plan of the structure with wide stairs and halls and oversized rooms restricted the housing capacity in marked contrast to the volume of the building.

There was but one guest room, and this was already occupied by a visiting Chinese Dominican. Later on, the fathers would help me to get located in a nearby hotel.

In the simple refectory, over a humble dinner, I met the cheerful community of half a dozen Irish priests and was made to feel very much at home. They were pleased with the statue and eager to assist in forwarding my plans.

There was no telephone in the house. A lay brother went out to call the cardinal's home, the patriarchate. The cardinal was out at the time. The brother left a message that I wished to call on him. He later sent word back that I could see him directly, but it was too late; I had already left with one of the priests, Father Gannon, for the afternoon.

We first went to visit an American warship, the cruiser *Spokane*, which was docked in Lisbon on a goodwill tour. We were kindly received by the chaplain and entertained in the wardroom and then shown about the ship. It seemed strange so soon after arriving in Portugal, to be again in the midst of Americans.

We had tea at the home of an English Catholic couple, Mr. and Mrs. Guy Wainewright. Their apartment was high on a hill, and from their living room we could look out over a picturesque maze of red tile roofs that rolled down before us and upward in the distance to the ancient Moorish section of the city.

Father Gannon first disposed of Existentialism; then the conversation turned to Fatima. The devout interest of the Wainewrights in all that pertained to Fatima made for lively conversation. We talked of Lucy, of the revelations, of the prayers taught by the angel and by our Lady, and of miracles. I was particularly interested in their eyewitness account of the miracle of the doves, the incident (to be detailed later) of December 1946 in which three white doves attached themselves to the famous statue of Our Lady of Fatima and remained with it for many days during a great religious celebration.

It was raining when we left for home. The long, curving, cobblestoned hill down which we walked was for some distance lined with large, attractive white apartment buildings. At a turn in the street, near the bottom, the picture changed suddenly to a sinister spectacle of ill-lighted barrooms that opened full front onto the sidewalk. The strong fumes of wine and tobacco issued around the forms of indolent patrons who seemed to be more shadows than persons. This was the seaport's center of vice. My companion commented that, although he understood there had been improvement in the moral conditions of the city, he believed that the previous state must have been extremely bad.

Back at Corpo Santo we were on time for Matins and Lauds in the balcony choir of the small church adjoining the monastery. Over coffee, after supper, there was a discussion of modern art. I would have preferred talking about Fatima, but I felt it unwise to press the subject. Art, therefore, was not an unwelcome substitute. I found myself engaged in defending, against much opposition, the virtue of modern art in its basic direction toward formal perfection.

Fatima finally came to the fore quite naturally. I had become accustomed to ignorance of Fatima, and also to a measure of indifference among those who knew something about it. In fact, I had gone through those stages myself. But it was now rather surprising to meet a peculiar sort of skepticism in those who, I thought, should have been better informed.

"We have Lucy," said one of the fathers. "Why do we need the pope?" He was referring ironically to what seemed to him a complication of devotion brought about by Fatima. He seemed to resent the novelty that he regarded as inherent in such things as the Communions of reparation of the Five First Saturdays, the consecration of Russia to the Immaculate Heart, and the prayers revealed by an angel and by our Lady.

As might be expected in a discussion among Irishmen on any topic other than the articles of faith, there was division of opinion. Some argued, as I did, that our position on Fatima must be determined not by our preferences but by facts. The important question is not whether we like the revelations of Fatima, but whether there were true revelations at Fatima.

For years the fathers had been quite familiar with the original data of Fatima, some from the very beginning, in 1917. No one doubted the fact of our Lady's apparitions. The miracle of the sun was beyond question. For twenty-five years they had been inspired by the fact that our Lady had come to Portugal, that her coming had revived the faith of the people, that she had given great force to the apostolate of the Rosary, that she had asked for penance.

Suddenly, in 1942, a complexity of details was revealed. Devotion to the Immaculate Heart must be established. Russia must be consecrated to the Immaculate Heart. The devotion of the Five First Saturdays must be propagated. Further, it was said for the first time that an angel had appeared to the children in 1916 and that prophecies of the past war and other afflictions had been made in 1917. All this was new; it seemed startling, confusing, and, in a sense, unnecessary.

Different reports gave conflicting details; no completely clear exposition of the entire revelations and chronology of Fatima seemed to be at hand.

Detachment from recently divulged and inadequately explained revelations seemed to be the best safeguard of Fatima's original simplicity. Fatima was close to the fathers of Corpo Santo, and the Fatima of 1917 was an absolute certainty. But this very familiarity was the hindrance that familiarity often is to investigation.

The recent revelations had come from Lucy. There was no question of her integrity, but there was some wonder about her ability, after thirty years and so many questionings, to be perfectly clear on all that had happened in 1917. And was it safe to credit the alleged reports of what she had made known?

One important conclusion issued from this evening's interchange of views—it was important to seek further light on all the points debated. For this reason, Father Gerard Gardiner was appointed to accompany me to Fatima and Oporto. He would not only assist me as interpreter but would also bring back information for the community of Corpo Santo. In recalling this development, I am reminded that, after living many years in New York City, I first visited the Statue of Liberty when a friend of mine came from California.

The evening was not devoted entirely to Fatima and art. Among lighter topics, my American accent was given critical but good-natured comment by my Irish brethren. Having their blood, if not their brogue, I replied in kind and demanded, "The question is: Who has the accent?" I insisted that the pure American accent, free of regional pronunciations, is superior to the rendition given our mother tongue in any country in the world.

It was late when the gathering broke up. Father McVeigh guided me through a cold drizzle about two blocks to a hotel. After I checked in, a bellboy conducted us to a nearby building, part of which was apparently used by the hotel as an annex. Up several flights of creaky stairs we arrived at a landing. The boy unlocked a door that led into a dimly lit hallway, off which there were half a dozen rooms. Father said good night and left. Then, to my amazement, the boy turned the key in the lock of the hallway door. Yes, I was locked in, and I would have to use the hall telephone when I wanted to get out.

The room was clean, but it was an icebox. I sat on the bed, still wearing my topcoat, to say my Office by the light of a small, unshaded bulb.

A few notes on the happenings of the day, and I would retire. The chill that I felt many times during my stay in Portugal was now severe. It was among the first impressions recorded: "Feel like going to bed with clothes on." There was a review of incidents, then of reflections on them, of mixed reactions to persons, places, and ideas, of the relation of such things to Fatima.

Before retiring I opened the French doors and stepped out on the balcony. A few stragglers were standing outside a tavern across the street several stories below. The city was quiet except for the honking of horns now and then that came up from the Cais do Sodré down the hill. The cavernous side streets were still and dark.

My initial idea emerged in definite deed. The final note in the diary for February 1 reads: "To bed—with clothes on!"

3

PERMISSION

Sunday brought freedom. The hall phone worked; the door was unlocked; and I left the little hotel annex forever.

Lisbon was interesting, and the fathers were good company; but Lucy was still as far away as she had been the day before, and so was the ecclesiastical permission to visit her. The community of Corpo Santo had little rest on this day of rest until Father Gannon accompanied me to the patriarchate.

The taxi ride brought us through two or three miles of the city's colorful streets and up a hill to a wide stone building that faced out on a small park. The patriarchate, I learned, had housed the German embassy before the First World War.

The cardinal was not at home. A kindly, white-haired monsignor assured me that he would arrange an interview as soon as possible and notify me by mail. Another day would have to pass!

Incidentally, the monsignor was not overwhelmed by the beauty of my little statue.

On the way back, Father Gannon introduced me to the Stilwell family, English friends of the Dominicans of Corpo Santo.

Mrs. Stilwell and several of her many grown children who were at tea liked the statue and made a place for it on their mantle during my visit. All were greatly devoted to Our Lady of Fatima and showed special interest in my project. From them, as from the fathers, I heard much of the extraordinary expressions of devotion and penance that characterize the pilgrimages at the Cova da Iria. They, too, described and made known added details of the incident of the doves.

An interesting fact came to light regarding the miracle of the sun of October 13, 1917. Mrs. Stilwell said that her aunt, a Portuguese lady who had died a few days before, was present at the miracle and that, although she saw the effect of the miracle on the crowd—that is, their kneeling and making acts of faith and contrition—she observed nothing extraordinary in the sky apart from the sudden cessation of the heavy rain.

I asked Mrs. Stilwell whether her aunt had said anything about the reported remarkable drying out of people's clothes after the miracle. She replied that this phenomenon was quite common at Fatima! The wonders of Fatima seem to be almost commonplace to the faithful of Portugal and accepted quite matter-of-factly.

This same attitude toward the miraculous was manifest among the fathers, at evening recreation. They recognized, of course, the necessity of proving the revelations of Fatima with evidence of miracles and my reason for inquiring so much about the subject. They were well acquainted with the Fatima wonders but seemed to find them as unexciting as ordinary, nonmiraculous, religious experience. In fact, my curiosity was subjected to their good-humored ridicule. I was jokingly accused of being a "miracle monger" by Father Gardiner.

"By the way, I performed a miracle, you know," he said.

"Is that so? Tell me about it."

He did! A woman suffering from Pott's disease had arranged to receive Holy Communion in an ambulance on her way to the hospital and to be blessed with a relic of Saint Philomena. She was completing a novena to Saint Philomena on that day. Father Gardiner gave her Holy Communion and blessed her. On her arrival at the hospital, the woman was found to be cured, her skeleton fully restored. The woman's devotion to Saint Philomena had been inspired by another priest of Corpo Santo, Father Paul O'Sullivan, famed for his apostolic zeal through fifty-two years of priestly ministration in Lisbon. Father O'Sullivan said that he had the before and after X-ray plates that proved the miracle.

More to my purpose, Father Gardiner told me of having seen at Fatima a girl who had been bedridden for years rise and adore the Blessed Sacrament. I was later to learn more of this case, to meet the girl, and to gather proofs of her cure.

Father Gardiner then related an experience of his first visit to Fatima during a pilgrimage. A man had asked to go to confession. Sitting on a rock, Father Gardiner heard him. Another followed, and another, and on until he had been there for four hours. He remarked that after that, no miracles were needed to convince him of the truly supernatural character of Fatima, so great had the conversions been!

The victrola was played during this recreation. First, there were several Irish songs, then some records of Marian Anderson.

"How do you defend the treatment of Negroes in the States?" I was asked.

"I don't," I answered. I think there was disappointment among those Irishmen at seeing a perfectly good argument go begging.

Word of my appointment with the cardinal came, at last, the next day. Father Gardiner accompanied me to do the interpreting. A cold, driving rain fell all afternoon.

After a dash from the taxi into the patriarchate, with box and briefcase, we ascended a great marble staircase, under the inspection of the portraits of Lisbon's past archbishops, and entered through an anteroom into the main reception room. A floor about thirty by sixty feet was mostly open but for a small, marble-topped table, and uncovered but for large bear and tiger rugs. Furnishings were few, and Renaissance in character. There was, beside a divan where we waited, a small red plush chair with a footrest of the same color and material.

I had brought with me no impressions of Cardinal Cerejeira's appearance but felt that with the name of patriarch there would be accompaniments of age and frailty. Instead, an alert, handsome man of medium stature and vigorous middle age entered. He received us with seriousness, which became his dignity, and with kindness, which put us completely at ease.

The letter of introduction from Cardinal Spellman had preceded us; the principal purpose of the visit was speedily achieved, the cardinal graciously assented to write an introduction for me to the bishop of Leiria.

Besides wishing to obtain criticism of the statue, I explained, it was my hope to be able to inquire into some Fatima problems that had been perplexing to many persons in the United States. The patriarch stated that the bishop of Leiria, in whose jurisdiction the Sanctuary of Fatima exists, was the proper one to reply to my questions.

He remarked that he had never visited Lucy. He explained that he felt it was not his province and therefore that he had no curiosity to meet her. But he gave evidence that he deeply respected her and fully accepted her testimony.

The cardinal dwelt on some of the post-1917 developments of Fatima. He said that after the pastoral of the bishop of Leiria in 1930, which declared the apparitions of Fatima to be worthy of credence, the one corporate act of the hierarchy of Portugal, based on the words of Lucy, was the consecration of Portugal to the Immaculate Heart, in 1931.

He then gave the explanation of Lucy's memoirs. In 1935, he said, when the body of Jacinta was exhumed and found incorrupt, the bishop sent a photograph taken of Jacinta's body to Lucy. Lucy, in return, wrote a letter extolling the virtue of her little friend and declaring her conviction of Jacinta's sanctity. This aroused the bishop's curiosity—perhaps many graces given to the children had been hidden all these years. He therefore commanded Lucy to write her memoirs. These memoirs are the substantial source of all the information about Fatima that Lucy had kept to herself and only reluctantly, at the command of her religious superior, the bishop of Leiria, has divulged.

The problem of prophecy in relation to the Secret of Fatima was next submitted to His Eminence. In the Secret of Fatima there is a definite prediction of World War II made to Lucy by the Blessed Virgin in 1917 but not made known publicly until the war was already well under way. Is there evidence, I inquired, that prediction of the war was made known by Lucy before the event?

The cardinal smiled in recognition of the difficulty, saying, "Yes, it would appear very easy to predict the war in 1942." He replied with certain evidences of Lucy's having made predictions in advance of the events. For instance, he said that in the early part of February 1939, he received a copy of a letter that the bishop of Leiria had received from Lucy. He gave the substance of this letter in the following words, which, he said, were very close to the actual text: "War is imminent. The sins of men will soon be washed in their own blood. Those nations will suffer most in this war which tried to destroy the Kingdom of God. Portugal will suffer some of the consequences of war, but because of the consecration of Portugal to the Immaculate Heart, the country will be saved from the horrors of war."

The important address of Pope Pius XII to the Portuguese people made in Portuguese on October 31, 1942, in connection with the ceremonies of the silver jubilee of the apparitions at Fatima was evidently, His Eminence pointed out, a consequence of Lucy's request made to the Holy Father, of which the cardinal had knowledge. Lucy had said that the Blessed Virgin wanted the world consecrated to her Immaculate Heart with special mention to be made of Russia. She had declared that the special grace to be granted in reward for this consecration would be the shortening of the war, and that, if the Holy Father wished to see an example of the blessings that this would bring to the world, it could be observed in the case of Portugal.

The cardinal, in reply to my inquiry, said that he had not heard of the special manner of consecrating Russia to the Immaculate Heart, which had lately been declared; namely, that all the bishops of the world are expected to participate with the Holy Father on a special day in one great act of offering Russia to our Lady's Immaculate Heart.

Our conversation on Fatima concluded with these words of His Eminence: "For me the mission of Fatima in the world is similar to that of Paray-le-Monial.[2] What Paray has been for the devotion of the Sacred Heart, Fatima will be for the devotion of the Immaculate Heart of Mary."

[2] Paray-le-Monial is the site of the apparitions of Jesus to Saint Margaret Mary Alacoque, whom He asked to promote devotion to His Sacred Heart.—Ed.

Father Gardiner and I left the next morning for Leiria.

There was an air of excitement in the Estação Rocio. Although one cannot go very far in Portugal, traveling of any kind is a rare experience for most Portuguese. The wheezing and clanging of small locomotives resounded from tiled walls, as passengers threw basket valises up the high steps of cars and clambered aboard.

The train moved slowly out of the station and continued to move slowly out of Lisbon into the open country. This part of Portugal that borders the ocean is rough terrain. Vegetation is sparse, for it must survive the scorching summer winds from Spain and the wintry blasts from the Atlantic. Woods of sea pines are seen along the way. They were introduced centuries ago to conserve the soil from the inroads of the coastal sand dunes. Walls of loose stones frame rolling farms of grape and corn and olive.

There were many stops. Each station was long and low and white, trimmed artistically with figured patterns of light blue ceramic tile. Automobiles were scarce; the unpaved streets between rows of whitewashed buildings were traveled mostly by oxcarts, horses, and overladen donkeys.

In about three hours we were at the station marked "Leiria," which happens to be a good distance from the city. Passengers piled into an old red bus as men worked noisily throwing produce, parcels, valises, and bags of mail on its roof.

Leiria is a flat city of white and ocher buildings, marked impressively by a steep cliff that rises abruptly from its center, crowned with the parapets of an ancient Moorish castle.

At an open square we came to the episcopal residence, a simple two-story building of light-tan stucco. We went up a worn wooden stairway to the bishop's apartment on the second floor.

A small throne occupied the center of the reception room and was covered with muslin, as were the other chairs, which went around the walls. Pictures of Fatima crowded the walls. I inspected these distractedly as I paced up and down waiting for the bishop.

His Excellency, the Most Reverend Dom José Correia da Silva, Bishop of Leiria-Fatima, the prelate on whose decision depended the fulfillment or failure of my hope, entered slowly and painfully, aged and obese. His lameness was evidence of torture that he had endured in the anticlerical persecutions of the Portuguese revolution. Childlike sweetness marked a habitual smile and somewhat relieved the tenseness that both Father Gardiner and I experienced.

Father Gardiner spoke rapidly in clear-cut Portuguese that I could follow because I was so familiar with the subject. He explained the origin of my trip and the intention of my proposed visit to Lucy. During this explanation His Excellency studiously regarded first one, then the other of us. He must have given my petition grave thought, but he replied simply, as if merely assenting to an unimportant request, with a nod and the all-important "Yes."

Encouraged by this success, I had Father Gardiner ask if I might have the privilege of a second visit with Lucy. I explained that there might be minor changes recommended in the statue by Lucy, and these I wished to express in drawings that I would show for her approval on the second visit. The bishop said that this would be all right with him, if it met with the approval of Lucy's mother provincial.

I showed him the statue. He apologized for the comment that the face of our Lady looked too old.

The bishop remarked that he knew Lucy did not like the statue at the Sanctuary, which is so greatly venerated, but added that the people did and, therefore, it could not be changed. He himself apparently is greatly attached to that image not only because of its typical Portuguese character but particularly because of the profound impression it had made upon the people of Portugal and its intimate association with Our Lady of Fatima throughout the years when Lucy, because of her seclusion, was unable to pass judgment upon any image of Our Lady of Fatima.

Despite the cold and rain, this was a most beautiful day. Now my hope was certainly to be fulfilled. I would see Lucy.

4

FATIMA

We mapped out our plans at a late lunch in the quiet dining room of Leiria's hotel. Lucy was at Vila Nova de Gaia, which is near Oporto. We found that no train from Leiria to Oporto would fit in with a visit to Fatima. We would have to get the express, or *Rápido*, on the side of the mountains beyond Fatima. In order to avoid an extra trip, we had to call again on the bishop in the afternoon to get the letters necessary for the interview.

The rain had let up. Outside the bishop's residence an orator had attracted a small crowd. We could hear his harangue as we waited for the bishop in the reception room. You would think, from the force of his delivery, that he was stirring up a revolution, rather than expounding the blessings of a patent medicine.

The bishop wrote two letters: one to the rector of the seminary in Oporto; the other to Lucy's mother provincial.

I asked if I might submit a few questions about Fatima. His Excellency consented.

Recently, there had been reports in the United States that the use of the scapular was part of the devotional message of the

Blessed Virgin at Fatima. Lucy and the bishop had both been quoted in support of this view. Were the reports accurate?

The bishop replied, "I never spoke of the scapular."

"What, then, are the devotions recommended by our Lady at Fatima?" I asked.

The bishop answered that, in his opinion, there were three devotions recommended by our Lady: the Rosary, devotion to Our Lady of Mount Carmel, and devotion to Our Lady of Sorrows, in that order of importance. He regarded these as the means toward fulfillment of the purpose of Fatima, which is amendment of life.

"Why have we heard only of the Rosary?" I inquired.

"The Rosary," said the bishop, "is the essential Fatima devotion." He added that the others have been spoken of and are secondary.

During the miracle of the sun, on October 13, 1917, after our Lady's appearance over the tree, Lucy had seen a series of apparitions: Saint Joseph and the Christ Child beside our Lady, our Lord as a man, Our Lady of Mount Carmel, and Our Lady of Sorrows. In the light of the interviews I later had with Lucy, I suppose that the bishop interprets the apparitions of our Lady under those aspects as recommendation of the corresponding devotions.

There is a basic unity among all Marian devotions. Whatever titles or forms of veneration may be used, all are directed to the person of our Lady; and the merits to which we pay honor all stem from the one radical excellence of her divine maternity.

The bishop, I thought, aptly disposed of the problem of devotional multiplicity when he said, "Our Lady cannot be in competition with herself under various titles. There is only one 'Our Lady.'"

The memoirs of Lucy, source of practically all the vital information on Fatima, should contain the answers to questions of Fatima facts and interpretations. I asked the bishop why these memoirs could not be published in their entirety. The bishop answered that the important memoirs had already been published in the book *Jacinta*, by Father Galamba, and that the only parts of her memoirs not published were private letters.

I happened to have a copy of the book he mentioned, in my briefcase. When the bishop said that he would like to have a copy of the English translation, I gave him mine. I countered with a request for a copy of the historical pastoral letter of 1930, in which he had declared the credibility of the 1917 apparitions. He regretted not having a copy in English but said he would give me one in Portuguese.

This brought us into his large study. He showed us several shelves of books on Fatima written in many languages. He told us that the official paper of the Sanctuary, *A Voz de Fátima* (*The Voice of Fatima*), had attained the highest newspaper circulation in Portugal without any promotion of subscriptions.

There had been some seminarians in the hallway downstairs. I wanted to get their reaction to my statue. The bishop obligingly sent for them. I like to think that their silence after viewing the statue was due to reverent familiarity with the conventional image, rather than to their kindness. One ventured a mild expression of satisfaction with the statue's simplicity.

When we went down the stairs from his apartment to set out for Fatima, the bishop was amiably receiving his next caller — a tattered beggar.

Returning to the hotel to get our baggage, we had to hurry through a cloudburst. The shower held us in the small lobby. A swarthy salesman with a garish blanket over his arm had had no success with the clerk and a few loiterers, so he directed his efforts toward us. A few words in Portuguese and immobile indifference from Father Gardiner turned him to me as his last hope at the hotel.

"*Não falo Português*," I pleaded. But he was unconvinced, and, to the amusement of all, he loosed on me a barrage of pleas and recommendations, until I gave him a coin. He accepted the money without thanking me; then, in fury at my blindness to a bargain, stomped out of the hotel.

Fatima is about fifteen miles southeast of Leiria, on the top of a mountain range called the Serra d'Aire. The approach to the Serra is an asphalt road that winds and curves over hilly country. The rain had stopped, and bright sunlight had broken through the clouds, heightening the colors of fields, trees, rock walls, and white houses.

We stopped to see the famous Monastery and Church of Our Lady of Victory in Batalha. From here Dominicans had gone forth for centuries to preach the Rosary. The devotion had survived persecution in the homes of the faithful people of this hill country.

The monastery, where three hundred friars had once lived, was now deserted but for a sentinel who stood guard at the tomb of Portugal's Unknown Soldier of the First World War. A collection of trophies of that war filled what once was the chapter hall.

Tabernacle veil and sanctuary lamp in a side chapel indicated the presence of the Blessed Sacrament. The new government of Portugal had restored the church to its rightful purpose.

Sculptors were busy in many chapels replacing fragments of carvings, damaged by the ages, along the flutings of the arches.

The Batalha church, regarded by many as one of the finest Gothic churches of Europe, has a rare balance of solid design and delicate ornamentation.

The climb up the Serra d'Aire is steep. There is a thinning out of trees at the roadside; houses are fewer; and the verdure fades toward gray on the rock-filled slopes. At a curve on the mountainside we looked back on the cottages of a village huddled in the valley. Beyond, the rolling landscape spread out for miles toward the plains, in the direction of the sea.

The first sign of Fatima was a stone cross, tall and unadorned. It bore the numeral 1. It was the first station of Fatima's Way of the Cross, which extends over two and a half miles to the Sanctuary. Father Gardiner told me that pilgrims making the Stations can be seen by the hundreds on pilgrimage days, going the entire distance on their knees.

Nearing Fatima we saw a rainbow made of two great arches. The ends seemed to be touching the fields and moving along parallel with the car. The tall tower of Fatima's basilica came into view at times over the hills, white against the dark sky. The clouds were very close to this lonely, unsheltered plateau on top of the mountain.

"Cova da Iria" was painted in yellow on a black road sign. Before us, on either side of the straight, level road for half a mile were rows of two- and three-story stucco buildings, white, ocher, pink, blue. Occasionally their plain surfaces were relieved by small window balconies of iron. They were religious houses, inns, homes, and shops—all built since 1917.

A trip to the Fatima shrine was probably uneventful for our driver. He did not slow up as we went by the tall stone wall at the roadside near the entrance of the village that ornaments the south rim of the Cova. I had only a glimpse of the great hollow with its basilica and hospitals.

We stopped at a green wooden building near the edge of the village, an inn called Pousada de Nossa Senhora do Rosário da Fátima. Mr. Petracchi, the proprietor, welcomed us. I tried speaking to him in Italian, but learned that despite his name and appearance he was English and about as familiar with Italian as I was with Gaelic. He showed us through the dining room, which occupied the front of the building, to our rooms, off the narrow hall that divided the remainder of the one-story structure. There was no heating. The cold, the unpainted woodwork, and the springless beds confirmed the reputation of severe simplicity that visitors remark of Fatima. There are no luxuries and few comforts at this shrine of penance.

The few peasants along the road, as others I had seen on the way from Leiria, were short and sturdy of stature, with firm, regular features. They were poorly and somberly clothed. Women wore black dresses and veils, and, along with their children, were generally barefoot; the men had well-worn suits, usually brown or gray, collarless shirts, and nearly always the *boné*, a long, black stocking cap that falls to the shoulder.

Gathering impressions of the people in the vicinity of Fatima, I found that curiosity was unilateral. This might have been because they are accustomed to visitors from many lands; but my feeling, borne out in future contacts, was that, beyond their black eyes, there are self-assured and independent personalities. They have wrested a living from the stubborn soil of the Serra, and in the process they seem to have acquired a strange likeness to their surroundings: austere, solid, and uncommunicative. They were always courteous but never obsequious; friendly, but reserved.

The panorama of the Sanctuary of Our Lady of the Rosary of Fatima fans out to the north at the west end of the village. It is dominated by the graceful spire of the basilica, which rises more than two hundred feet on the hill, about a quarter of a mile from the road. The church is made of a cream-colored stone, lighter than the other buildings, and stands as on a pedestal on a great stairway that leads down to the saucer-shaped hollow. Beneath the cross, a dark-green bronze crown tops the mounting movement of the tower. There is an empty niche over the doorway. Scaffoldings made of rough logs were leaning against the sides of the huge nave. The tower was standing out against a magnificent billowing cloud that had been turned a red-gold in the light of the setting sun.

We went through the gateway, down a wide gravel walk, toward the fountain, which is the hub of the Cova. To the right and left of the walk, retaining walls drop down to irregular depressions, which are sprinkled with small trees and rough rock formations. These quarter segments of the circle are the only unaltered remains of the original Cova.

The fountain in the center is a gray circular stone structure, surrounded by arches, from whose roof a column rises to sustain a gilded statue of the Sacred Heart. Between the fountain and the basilica is the expansive semicircle of sandy, graded fill, where the hundred thousands gather on the days of pilgrimage.

On the right, the shell of a new hospital was rising; the old hospital is on the ridge to the left. Beyond it, and not seen from the Cova, is the hospice, which is used for retreatants and for the offices of the Sanctuary.

However, I took note of the hospital, at first, only as the yellow background for a deep-red tile roof of a small structure about twenty yards up the slope from the fountain. The roof, at the far end, covers a tiny white-walled chapel with room enough for only the celebrant and a few worshippers; but most of the roof is over a porch of rough cement. This is the goal of every pilgrim's journey—the Chapel of the Apparitions. Outside and a little to the left of the doorway of the chapel, a stone column, seven feet high, marks the spot where the Blessed Virgin appeared to the children.

As we arrived at the steps in front of the chapel the great bells of the basilica were ringing out the Angelus.

5

LUCY'S SISTERS

The statue in the niche over the altar of the Chapel of the Apparitions was not the celebrated "miraculous statue" but a temporary replacement. The original statue of Our Lady of Fatima, the one carved by the Portuguese sculptor José Thedim, was in the hospital at the time being redecorated. While it was being carried in the month-long procession from Fatima to Lisbon and back again in December 1946, thousands of suppliant hands had touched and soiled it.

A lay brother brought us into the hospital to see the famous image. We met the artist who was doing the painting. The flesh-tones had been applied, but the remainder of the figure was all white. He had still to add the touches of gold to the carved ornamentation along the borders of the mantle and to the long cord and tassel that hung from the shoulders.

The statue is about three feet high and carved in Brazilian cedar. The hands are joined in an attitude of prayer; the head is tilted slightly to the left. Mantle, tunic, and a stole-like garment that shows within the borders of the mantle are very full and heavy-looking, as if the fabric were thick wool.

Whatever differences exist between the vision as described by Lucy and Senhor Thedim's statue, which had to be made without the benefit of Lucy's description, certain facts must be noted concerning this statue. It is perfectly carved. It is beautiful, especially because of the appealing loveliness and subtle pathos expressed in face and hands. It is the first statue ever made of Our Lady of Fatima. It has occupied the place of honor at Fatima since 1920. It is the best known and most venerated image in Portugal.

When the original chapel at the Cova was dynamited on May 6, 1922, everything was destroyed but the statue. Miracles have been reported as happening in connection with acts of veneration before it. In particular it was honored by the miracle of the doves in December 1946. Any or all of these facts may account for the popular designation "miraculous."

There is no reason for ever replacing this statue in the Chapel of the Apparitions. It has been solemnly crowned by a papal legate. It has represented our Lady for years at the spot where she appeared. But, although we must accept the statue for its traditional and popular importance, there is no need of copying and perpetuating the many details in which it differs from Lucy's description. The original statue must be kept in its place of honor, but, it seems to me, all future images of Our Lady of Fatima should conform to Lucy's very clear corrections.

Visitors from all over the world go to Fatima. On the morning after our arrival, an Irish-American priest from Brazil served my

Mass; the sacristan was an Italian; after breakfast I met a priest-author from Paris.

Later in the morning we were visiting with Mr. Petracchi in the dining room. I told him I would like to meet some of the people who had witnessed the happenings of 1917. The opportunity came quickly when he noticed that Lucy's sister, Teresa, was riding down the road on a donkey cart. He ran after her a long way to call her back.

Teresa came into the dining room of the Pousada. She was dressed all in black. A heavy veil that covered her hair was tied above her forehead in a bow. She sat quite erect at a table, agreeable but businesslike in submitting to the interview. Her eyes were dark, and the skin of her strong face was deeply tanned and furrowed.

I asked her to tell me something about the miraculous incidents of the apparitions.

She said that she was present at the July apparition and saw nothing, that in August she saw flowers resembling snow falling from the sky, and colored light like a rainbow on the ground. The people put out their hands to catch the flowers only to find that they disappeared. She explained that on that day the children were not present and that their father, Ti Marto, came to say that there was no need to wait; then the phenomena mentioned occurred. She said that in September there was nothing extraordinary noticeable; all that she heard were the voices of the children.

Then came her account of the October apparition and the miracle of the sun. She said that it had rained the whole morning. The rain stopped suddenly. Gradually the clouds cleared and the sun was visible; there was no eyestrain. Next, flowers again were "snowing," and there was a rainbowlike light all over the ground and the people. The people looked up to see where the light was coming from, and they saw the sun spinning around. She said they could look at it as at the "newly risen moon"; it was "spinning down."

Even after the last apparition she again saw the flowers and the lights on the thirteenth of November and in several following months. In November she deliberately looked at the ground, thinking the light might have caused the illusion of flowers and still she saw the flowers falling.

I inquired next about sounds at the scene of the apparitions. Teresa returned to the August events. Just after the father of Jacinta and Francis said that there was no use in staying, there was a terrific explosion "as if a bomb had exploded under our feet." The crowd, which she estimated at about two hundred to three hundred people, was frightened and ran toward the road. Then all stopped and asked each other what it was, took courage and returned. Then followed the phenomena of the flowers and lights.

I asked her when it was that Lucy first spoke of the miracle to be performed in October. Teresa said she thought it was in September.

I inquired if she spoke with Lucy about the apparitions. She replied that the family never asked questions.

"Why not?" I asked.

She answered, "They saw she didn't like it; she would run away."

According to Teresa, the family referred to the apparitions at the time, in speaking with Lucy, only by way of correction. Sometimes they would say, "You are the girl who saw our Lady, and then you do a thing like that." Lucy might be, for instance, dancing or singing.

"What would she answer?" I inquired.

"'There is no harm in it!'" Teresa explained that they were only joking with her.

"Did your mother object to Lucy's presence at the apparitions?" I asked.

Teresa replied, "My mother never believed in the apparitions, said they were quite impossible, until the final apparition in October."

"Did you tell her what happened in August?" I inquired.

"When we saw the happenings of August," she replied, "we told her and she said, 'It's ridiculous; you are all crazy.'"

Teresa explained that what brought her mother to the Cova in October was not the possibility of seeing anything to make her believe, but fear inspired by a report that the children would be taken away and killed. In October she saw the wonders and then became convinced.

Again, back to the miracle of the sun:

"In October did the sun spin around several times and then fall?"

She replied, "No, it spun around a very short time, and as it was spinning it seemed to fall, and there was a shower of flowers."

I asked, at this point, what the flowers appeared to be.

She said they were multicolored petals, but when they came close enough to see what they were, they disappeared.

Teresa was inclined to minimize the numbers present at the apparitions preceding the miracle of the sun in October. When I cited the numbers of thousands reported in books I had read, she said, with a firmness reminiscent of accounts of her mother's staunch veracity, "I believe in telling the truth even when it is not sensational, even when I must disappoint people."

Teresa had given us very generously of her time, and we readily excused her when she pleaded that she had chores to do at home. We told her that we were going to see her sister at the convent in Vila Nova de Gaia. Dutifully and unemotionally, Teresa asked us to greet Lucy for her.

Then she went out, climbed up beside her husband on the cart, and the two drove off to their home in Aljustrel.

Aljustrel, where the children lived in 1917, is about a mile and a half southeast of the Cova da Iria and half a mile south of the village of Fatima.

Everyone speaks of the Cova as Fatima. Actually the village of Fatima is about two miles east of the Cova. The name Fatima has been associated with the apparitions from the beginning because it was the parochial village of the neighborhood.

In the afternoon we went with Mr. Petracchi to see the village of Aljustrel and the homes of the children, and to meet Lucy's other sister, Maria.

Short of the village of Fatima we took a rocky lane to the right, which brought us, after another half mile or so, to Aljustrel. The narrow road curves in an S north to south and then dips down a steep hill. Along this road and quite close to it are the homes of the peasants, perhaps twenty in all. Most of them were one-story and were covered with stucco, usually cream color. Some were ornamented in deep blue and green. Each house had a chimney that terminated in a standard covering of Moorish design with little S-shaped slots all around the top. Children were running about barefoot, their clothes worn and soiled. Burros with loads of sticks or brush leaves were being prodded along the road. Near the end of the village, we arrived at Maria's house. It is the house in which Lucy was born.

The door opened into a small, central room, to the left and rear of which were the bedrooms, and to the right the weaving room and kitchen. A little table was at one wall, and above it were various religious articles.

Maria was genial and smiled very sweetly at our coming. She declined to sit, preferring to lean on the table as both Mr. Petracchi and Father Gardiner interpreted my questions and her answers.

She said that nobody from Aljustrel went to the June apparition, only some from other places. As far as she knew, nothing extraordinary was observed, only the behavior of the children.

She estimated the group in July at one hundred. She saw Lucy talking and listening as one does in conversation. Maria and others heard a sound like a "bee buzzing around inside an iron jar." She remarked on this to her sister Teresa, but Teresa had not heard it. I asked her if she noticed the tree bending down at any time, and she said no.

Of the August instance she gave this account: Lucy was at the house ready to go to the Cova when the administrator came and asked if he could take the children to the priest's house to question them. The parents went along with them to the rectory. After the interrogation the administrator said he would bring the children to the Cova in his mule buggy. With this ruse he got them in the buggy and drove them to the Vila Nova d'Ourem.

Maria joined the crowd at the Cova. "After waiting some time, they became impatient," Maria went on. "They began to say there was no use waiting. Some said they heard a noise like sticks hitting together and ran away. Although I did not hear the noise, I ran with them up the north slope of the Cova to where the basilica now stands. I heard an old man say, 'People of little faith, don't you see it is a miracle?' Then I stopped running, returned, and saw the signs." Maria described the rainbow lights and falling flowers in about the same way as did Teresa. She remarked that they saw "clouds around the sun reflecting different colors on the people." Some saw the figure of our Lady in the clouds; she did not.

On the nineteenth of August, Maria continued, the children had returned from jail and were pasturing their sheep at Valinhos. "Mother was staying here," said Maria. "Jacinta came and said, 'O Aunt, our Lady has appeared again,' and showing a branch, 'These are the places where she put her feet.'" According to Maria, Lucy's mother then said to Jacinta, "I thought the administrator had finished with all that, and here you are still telling lies. I know what you need."

Here I asked if the children had been threatened with death by the administrator. Maria said yes. She continued to quote her mother speaking to Jacinta: "Now give me that thing and go back with Francis and Lucy and look after the sheep."

As Maria's mother took the branch, she noticed a scent and remarked to her, "A very pleasant odor, but it's not like roses or incense or perfume; I don't know what it is." She put it on the table intending to ask someone else if they could recognize the scent and left the room to go on with her work. In the evening she wanted to show the branch to others. It was gone. She asked everyone, but no one had seen it. She had been in the house all the time. Her belief in the apparitions began in October when at the Cova she sensed that same fragrance at the moment when Lucy said, "Close your umbrellas; here comes our Lady." The scent remained all the while Lucy was talking to our Lady. Maria commented that she herself did not smell this fragrance.

Maria then told this little story that I had not read before: A neighbor, who was Lucy's godmother, was also skeptical of the Cova apparitions and was out working in the fields when the apparitions took place at Valinhos on the nineteenth of August. Coming along the way she said to her sister, "There are those same lights they talked about on the thirteenth. If this were the thirteenth they would say this was the apparition of our Lady." On arriving in Aljustrel she heard the story of the apparitions at Valinhos. Maria's mother said to her, "Have you heard Jacinta has been here and said our Lady appeared again?" The woman who had doubted was greatly shocked. She then told what she had said to her sister.

On September 13 the soldiers came to guard the roads to the Cova, said Maria. Many people went to the Cova, and the soldiers chased them through the fields, but there were too many to cope with. Maria did not go, both because of the troops and because she had to take care of her small baby.

At home, at about two o'clock she heard horses' hoofs. She went out to see what it was and saw Lucy walking down the lane guarded from behind by two horse soldiers. When this strange procession arrived at the door, one of the soldiers asked, "Are you anything to this child?" "Yes," said Maria, "her sister." "Then," continued the soldier, "you will be responsible for her; she is not to leave this house." He went away.

Maria asked Lucy, "Did they arrest you?" Lucy's reply was, "No. They wanted to take me home on horseback and I said I was able to walk; I have done it often before." Maria commented that Lucy did not speak much. That night her uncle, Jacinta's father, came and said a family was in his house to see the children. Lucy said that she would not go, she had been forbidden by the soldiers; but she went when she was assured by her uncle that the prohibition meant only going to the Cova.

Before coming to the matter of the October apparition and the miracle of the sun, I asked Maria if the practice of saying the family Rosary had existed at their home. She answered that they had said the family Rosary only in May and November. When Lucy said that our Lady wanted the Rosary daily, they began the daily family Rosary in October. She then quoted the report of what our Lady said as it was given to the crowd by Lucy after the October apparition:

"Our Lord is greatly offended and we must say the Rosary every day, and we must beg His pardon.

"The soldiers will be back soon from the War."

During the October apparition Maria was standing at the spot where the gateway now is. Her husband would not let her go down with the baby because the whole Cova and slope were covered with people. Maria reports the developments as follows:

"Lucy said, 'Close your umbrellas.' The rain stopped immediately, the sun could be seen, and the clouds were turned different colors—all the colors you could think of. Then the sun fell toward the earth, and people fell on their knees asking for mercy, thinking it was the end of the world. Afterward Lucy said, 'Look in that direction.' A man standing near me said he saw a figure, a very beautiful form between two lights."

The duration of the miracle, according to Maria, was about two minutes. I inquired if the sun came out afterwards in its normal brilliance. She said she did not remember.

I asked Maria about the existence or nonexistence of clouds or mist in front of the sun. Maria said, "No, there was no mist about the sun. There were clouds around the sun, but the sun was clear, and you could look at it as at the moon. The sun went back after falling suddenly." Asked if she noticed that her clothes dried quickly, she replied that they had been soaked and that when they got home, they noticed their clothes were dry. She did not remember how long a time had elapsed before she returned home.

She told me then of a man named Carlos Mendes, now president of the municipality of Torres Novas, who, after the October apparition, put Lucy on his shoulder and carried her out to the crowd, stood her on a rock and asked her to tell what the Blessed Virgin said.

Maria summed up the message of our Lady, conveyed by Lucy in October, as a warning that we must stop offending our Lord, ask pardon for our sins, and pray the Rosary. Also, there was a prediction that the war would soon be over.

At the end of our visit Maria gave me a small piece of wood for a souvenir. It was part of a branch of the azinheira tree on which our Lady had stood.

6

THE CHILD OF THE MOUNTAINS

There was much more to be done by way of research on Fatima. I wanted to interview other witnesses of the 1917 events and, although I had taken several photos, many more were needed to round out a pictorial record of the places important in the story of Fatima. But I would be back very soon, I thought, from Vila Nova de Gaia and have plenty of time for these activities. We had lingered long enough; now we must get on to Oporto.

We had planned our departure with allowance of sufficient time for an ordinary taxi to get to the station east of the Serra. But ours turned out to be no ordinary taxi. I am sure that it must have brought a group of pilgrims to the miracle of the sun in 1917. It labored along level stretches and upgrades with all the speed of a bicycle; and on downgrades, even the slightest, the driver turned off the ignition to save gas. Our route took us through Vila Nova d'Ourem, the place where the children were imprisoned in 1917, thence down into the valley. We reached the station in Chão de Maçãs in time to buy our tickets before the arrival of the *Rápido*. In fact, we had a few minutes to spare.

There was an azinheira tree across the tracks. I had seen none at the Cova or during our walks. In Providence, weeks before, I had spent hours in the Botany Department of Brown University trying to track down a specimen of the tree, so that I would have the proper type of leaf beneath the feet of the statue; but I had failed to arrive at certainty. So I plucked a branch of the tree at Chão de Maçãs to show Lucy for verification.

True to its name, the *Rápido* sped along comfortably over the distance of about two hundred miles to Oporto. The pleasant rolling country was dotted with vineyards. The vines, in even rows, pruned of all branches and turned black by the cold, had the shape and movement of tongues of flame. This seemed to be richer country than the coastal section we had passed through on our trip from Lisbon to Leiria.

In the dining car we looked across the way on hearing English spoken and saw a group of young men dressed in an odd assortment of clothing. We spoke with them and learned that they were British seamen who had survived a ship disaster a few days before, a fire in which twenty of their companions had lost their lives. The clothing had been given them by their rescuers. They were returning home through Spain and France.

Before coming to the Douro River we passed a freight train loaded with tree bark. I asked Father Gardiner what it was. "Cork," said he. I had never before seen cork in its original state. "What sort of a tree does it come from?" I asked him. He answered without inflection: "Cork trees." That was that; now I knew that the author of the story of Ferdinand the bull had not thought up the species. Of course, my friend could have said, "Cork oak," to spare me, or better still, "*Quercus suber*," but Father Gardiner is not the sparing kind when amusement is at stake.

The train moved across the Douro River with the caution of a tightrope walker, on a single-track span that seemed to be two hundred feet from the water. Before us, on the left, the city of Oporto, crowded with tier upon tier of tightly packed buildings, covered the cliff-like bank. On the right, terraced gardens and vineyards with tall, narrow homes in many colors cut up the steep bank in a picturesque pattern of steps. Full-beamed sailboats with high prows and square sails plied the river.

The first introduction we were to present was addressed to Father António Ferreira Pinto, rector of the Oporto seminary. As soon as we had settled our belongings in a hotel and had had a bootblack clean the red clay of the Serra d'Aire off our shoes, we took a taxi to the seminary. It was raining very hard. We had to descend a flight of steps at the square beside the cathedral, then cross a wide courtyard to reach the entrance of the building.

Father Pinto brought us into his study. He was an elderly man and seemed grave and preoccupied. I could not understand the conversation between him and Father Gardiner, and I became concerned when his tone and expression seemed negative. I wondered if, after the gracious reception by the patriarch and the promptly given permission of the bishop, we had run into a new authority with whom we had not reckoned, who could veto the visit with Lucy. Father Gardiner did not say a word in English to relieve the suspense. When he told me to show my statue to the rector, I had the feeling that I was trying to convince him that I really was a sculptor and had a good reason to see Lucy.

Not until we had left the rector's office did I learn the reason for his alarming expression.

He was so busy and the weather was so bad that he did not want to accompany us. We had anticipated his company merely as part of the formality required for a visit with Lucy. So we were not extremely disappointed with his refusal.

Vila Nova de Gaia is across the river from Oporto. It is a smaller city, mostly residential. After going a short distance on the broad avenue beyond the bridge, we turned off on a long winding road that passed through a section of high-walled villas into a more densely settled neighborhood.

The main building of Colégio do Coração Sagrado de Jesus do Sardão, an ocher building with a red roof, rather long and plain looking, appeared at the end of a street after a final turn.

The rain beat on us as we stood, ringing over and over a bell at the side of the impenetrable iron plates that made up the gate. A little nun, flurried with apologies, finally let us in and led the way hurriedly up a steep flight of steps to the entrance on the second floor. She explained that it was the feast of Saint Dorothy and that all the sisters were at choir in a remote part of the building.

Relieved of our wet hats and topcoats we were ushered into the parlor that was the terminus of the journey. An oval, marble-topped table was in the center. A long-leafed plant and a picture album took up most of the space. No room, I thought, for statue or notebook.

I took the statue from the box and tried it in various locations. It did not show to advantage anywhere. The window frames were low and gave unflattering light from beneath, and in every conceivable spot in the room it had to compete for attention with many more conspicuous objects. I gave up trying and rested it beside a lamp. Then I joined Father Gardiner in the occupation of keeping every square foot of rug not already weighted down firmly in contact with the floor.

When a nun appeared in the doorway, I thought for a moment it was Lucy; then I realized that her face was older than Lucy's could be. A lovely little lady named Mother Corte Real, provincial of the Dorothean Sisters in Portugal and Spain, introduced herself. She said that she had been expecting us from the day before. The bishop had telephoned to say that two Dominican fathers from the United States were coming. Father Gardiner pretended to be indignant at this slight of his nationality; then he explained our connection.

Mother Provincial must have noticed the nervousness that we were both striving very bravely to conceal. She tried to put us at our ease. "There is nothing to be disturbed about," she said. "Irmã Dores is very simple; she is a child of the mountains." She assured us that Lucy would willingly answer our questions. Then she went out.

With all my preparations and travels, with all the desire I had had to see Lucy, I think that at that moment I would have preferred to be in a comfortable chair in my mother's apartment in New York. In a moment there would walk across the threshold a woman who knew some of the secrets of Heaven, who had seen and talked with the Blessed Virgin, a person favored by God, it seemed to me, beyond all others living and charged by Him to be the instrument of a divine message to mankind. I had heard and read of those very close to God having the power to search hearts and being able to tell people of their faults. I thought of a friend who had said he did not envy me for this reason. Yet, there was, as there had been from the beginning, a conviction of rightness in what I was doing. Whatever the cost to me emotionally, whatever reaction Lucy might have to me as a person, I had sought this opportunity so that I might be of service to the cause of our Lady through my work in sculpture and in any other way open to me.

Mother Corte Real soon returned and with her came "the child of the mountains." As she entered the room I was conscious of her eyes more than of her general appearance. Her eyes are very dark, very penetrating. My ego was sustained in the presence of these two little women by the mere advantage of physical height; both seemed slightly under five feet. Irmã Dores leaned forward as we shook hands, looked me straight in the eye and smiled pleasantly. In a moment we were all seated, and the first interview began.

7

IRMÃ DORES AND THE APPARITION

From now on I am going to call Lucy "Irmã Dores." It is the name by which she is known in her community. *Irmã* (as I was later to learn) is Portuguese for "sister." *Dores* is derived from the surname of her former pseudonym, Maria das Dores, which was given to her by the bishop when she was placed in the orphanage as a child. Used for a first name, its only equivalent in English is Dolores, since "sorrows"—the meaning of the word as a common noun—is not a name in English.

Strangely, however, Irmã Dores, although never addressed as Irmã Maria Lucia, usually signs her name "Irmã Maria Lucia de Jesus"; when she signs her full name, it is "Irmã Maria Lucia de Jesus Rosa Santos." Still, at the Colégio do Sardão, she is always called just Irmã Dores.

Before I visited Sardão, I always thought of her as Lucy, the girl to whom the Blessed Virgin appeared at Fatima; since I have known her, I have always thought of her as Irmã Dores, the sister who lives in order to make the message of Our Lady of Fatima known to the world.

Father Gardiner first conveyed the greetings sent by Maria and Teresa. Irmã Dores thanked him and inquired after her sisters. It was now my turn to speak.

I started by telling her that the following day would be the centenary of the consecration of the United States to the Immaculate Conception and asking her to pray for my country. As she later did at such requests, she nodded humbly as if embarrassed and faintly said, "Yes."

Her expression was not easily identified. Her eyes were most attentive and always fixed upon the person who was speaking. There seemed to be both passive and active qualities in her attitude. She humbly attended on the completion of any question yet keenly studied the person and words of the questioner. Agility and strength of mind were reflected in her mobile, expressive mouth and large chin. She sat relaxed but leaning a little forward. Her hands were usually folded in her lap, but sometimes she extended the fingers, pressing the palms on her knees in a natural gesture of relaxation from the tedious examination. Her voice, thin and high-pitched, fell in rather monotonous cadences—a characteristic which I have observed of many Portuguese, in contrast with the more varied tonal articulation of other Latin peoples. On provocation she laughed with spontaneity and brevity, consistent with her fine sense of humor and lifelong characteristic of reserve.

The explanation of my visit was briefly made. I was a sculptor. I had been commissioned to make a statue of Our Lady of Fatima, and I wanted the representation to be accurate. I wished to obtain her description of the vision. To facilitate her description I had brought along a small model for her to criticize.

Irmã Dores had already seen the statue across the room. She had shown no reaction whatever. I supposed that this was due to her reverent attentiveness to anyone speaking and was not a sign of disapproval.

Very little light was coming into the room from the torrents outside. When the moment came for her to inspect the statue we all moved to the window. My hopes were sustained by remembering the many comments of approval that the statue had received from my family and friends. I felt that its artistic validity had been established by the judgment of my former teacher, Mr. Carl Milles: "The best statue you have ever made." Now I would have the most important opinion of all. "If she approves ..." I would know soon.

I held my work at the most favorable height for her to study it. A very long second followed in which all of us waited for her reaction. Wrinkles formed on her brow (and in my soul).

"*Não dá posicão*," she said. That was the first sentence of Portuguese I learned and one I shall never forget: "It's not the right position."

"The right hand should be raised and the left lower down," she continued. I knew she was speaking of the June apparition and hastened to explain that in the gesture portrayed I was not intending to be descriptive but symbolic. I was indicating in the position of the hands the devotional message of Fatima, namely, the Immaculate Heart and the Rosary.

She smiled at my apologetic, unable to gather the interest I had in symbolism; nothing could substitute for the reality with her, it was obvious. She simply repeated her first comment, "*Não dá posicão*."

During this discussion, Irmã Dores noticed the strap that had been around the box lying on the floor, where, in my haste and distraction, I had left it. Without interrupting the conversation, she picked it up, folded it neatly, and put it on the box.

"The garments in the statue are too smooth," she said, after we were all seated again and the statue was resting on the little marble-topped table. The fascination of speaking with someone who had seen and spoken with our Lady contended with the disappointment of her not approving the work sufficiently to keep me interested in further criticism.

Again an apologetic: "I knew from published descriptions that the vision was very brilliant. Now, it is impossible to express light in sculpture otherwise than by reflecting light from simple surfaces. That is why I made the garments so smooth."

"But the light was in waves and gave the impression of a garment with folds" (literally an undulated garment), she said. "She was surrounded by light and she was in the middle of light," she went on, confirming the truth of my previous observation about brilliance. Then she added:

"Her feet rested on the azinheira."

This was a shock. Was there no cloud? Every account and every image had indicated that there was. The problem of designing the cloud had been especially vexing during the modeling of this statue—how to make something that would suggest vapor and still be integrated in a solid composition. I had thought, finally, that I had solved the problem quite well in the little carpet-like cloud that had emerged beneath the feet of the figure. Did Irmã Dores now mean that there was no cloud? I asked her.

"The people spoke of a cloud, but I saw none. Our Lady's feet rested lightly on the tops of the leaves." I told her I was disappointed because I thought the cloud a very pretty form.

Next, an omission was observed: "She always had a star on her tunic." I had thought that was one of the mistakes in the conventional image. Well, that would easily be remedied. But then she added another detail, one I had not heard of:

"She always had a cord with a little ball of light," she said, indicating an imaginary pendant around the neck falling to about the waistline. It was this detail that was mistaken for a cord and tassel after the first investigations in 1917.

Irmã Dores seldom referred to the Blessed Virgin as *nossa Senhora*, or "our Lady," but generally used just the personal pronoun *ela*, or "she." But, as Father Gardiner pointed out later, she pronounced *ela* with an inflection of such reverence that it became quite restricted, as though, used in that manner, it could apply to no one but our Lady.

Further points of information about the dress of Our Lady of Fatima were brought out in Irmã Dores's answers to a series of questions: there were only two garments visible—a simple tunic and a long veil, or mantle; the tunic had no collar and no cuffs; there was no cincture or sash around the waist, although the tunic was drawn in at the waist. When I asked Irmã Dores about the width of the sleeves of the tunic, she tugged lightly at a sleeve of my coat and said they seemed to be about that wide.

To fill out the form inside the mantle beside the neck I had shown the hair of our Lady. Although I had no justification in any description, neither did I know of any objection. The device had two advantages: it made the face appear more youthful, and it eliminated what I considered an objectionable shadow. I inquired what Irmã Dores thought of it.

"I never saw the hair." That settled that!

The statue again reminded her of the June apparition. "She appeared as the Immaculate Heart in June only," she said; then getting her Rosary out of a pocket of her habit, she draped it over the palm of her right hand and joined her hands in the attitude of prayer, continuing, "In June she appeared at first as in the other apparitions, then she opened her hands." Irmã Dores demonstrated. Her right arm was extended, the forearm forward of the plane of her waist and elevated only slightly above the horizontal, the hand gently arched, palm downward. Her left hand was upturned near the center and close to her body with the fingertips a little below the waist. After carefully establishing this position (I made her hold it for a while so that I might study it), Irmã Dores held her right hand flat about two inches in front of her left breast to indicate the position at which the Immaculate Heart appeared, surrounded by thorns. I expressed surprise that the heart appeared out from the body, but she assured me that it was so. It was not so good for sculpture, I thought, but the consideration did not disturb me very much. I was too much interested in hearing her complete description.

"At the first and third apparitions she opened her hands like this," Irmã Dores said, assuming a position similar to that of the priest at Mass when he says "*Dominus vobiscum*," but with her hands a bit lower.

Next, I questioned her about the azinheira, or holm oak, on which our Lady had appeared. I showed her the sprig I had plucked from a branch at Chão de Maçãs and asked her if it was the type of tree on which our Lady had stood. She confirmed the specimen.

"Were the leaves as small as this?" (It would be better for design to have larger leaves; I would take the liberty anyway.)

"They were, because the tree was young and small. A young azinheira at that age is called a *carrasqueira*. It was a meter or so and was just my height."

Returning to the more important elements, I asked if there was any difference between the mantle and the tunic. "The mantle was a wave of light."

"Wasn't the tunic?"

"Yes."

"What then was the difference?"

"There were two waves of light, one on top of the other." Puzzling about the possibility of suggesting the lucidity of the apparition while making folds in the drapery, I became rather insistent on the necessity of keeping the drapery simple. I explained that each fold would create a shadow and that the cumulative effect of many shadows would be to darken the figure generally. Her reply was, "No matter what you do, you won't give the impression of the reality."

"Did our Lady have shoes or sandals?" I asked.

"I don't remember, because I think I never looked at her feet."

This at first seemed curious, since she had just said that our Lady's feet rested on the tops of the leaves. But one can observe the location and position of a figure without taking note of all its details.

"Did the leaves of the azinheira bend down?" (Witnesses of the children's ecstasies had made this observation.)

"The leaves did not bend."

"Was there a line of gold on the mantle?"

"It was like a ray of sunlight all around the mantle." Later, when I was working on the statue, she said that this ray around the mantle was like a thin thread.

"Did the face and hands and feet of our Lady have the color of light or the color of flesh?" (A dilemma, I thought, but I was immediately enlightened.)

"Flesh-colored light," she replied, "light that took on the color of flesh."

I came back then to the problem of showing or concealing the hair. Irmã Dores again declared that the hair was not visible.

"But," I argued, "if the mantle falls from the hairline, it will conceal not only the hair but the profile as well."

"Whatever the difficulties may be in representing our Lady," Irmã Dores replied, "I never saw the hair."

Later on at the hotel when we were checking our notes, Father Gardiner, commenting on this reply and on my insistence, remarked that Irmã Dores had said in effect: "I'm not going to change the vision just to satisfy a sculptor."

As a matter of fact, the problem of the profile was simply solved when it came to making the new statue. Since the apparition was clothed in light rather than fabric there was no need to have the mantle fall with gravitational logic; I simply curved the line back where necessary to reveal the profile.

"What was our Lady's expression?"

"Pleasing but sad; sweet but sad." (*Agradável mas triste; doce mas triste.*)

I then pointed to the statue and asked hopefully if the line of the mantle over the length of the figure was all right. In the first statue there was a long oval contour that I treasured.

Irmã Dores again failed me. "It seemed to be straighter," she said. "It was a thing all made of light and very light"—that is, in weight. Father Gardiner said she could have used the word *ethereal*—"but it fell straight down." Then she pointed to the lower part of the mantle on the little statue and said that it should be back farther. So much for the general lines of my composition!

"Was the clothing all white?"

"All white."

"Except for the cord and the star?"

"Yes. The cord was a more intense and yellow light."

I reminded her of the star.

"The light of our Lady was white, and the star was yellow."

I asked Father Gardiner to inquire if by "yellow" Irmã Dores meant the same as gold. Father Gardiner was sure that she did, but I insisted that he ask her anyway. It was fortunate that I did, for the question evoked a description that would have been beautiful if it had been carefully written rather than spoken spontaneously. I later checked my notes with his in Portuguese to get every word exact:

> No. Yellow!
>
> She was all of light. The light had various tones, yellow and white and various other colors. It was more intense and less intense. It was by the different tones and by the differences of intensity that one saw what was hand and what was mantle and what was face and what was tunic.

Some images of Our Lady of Fatima had shown our Lady to be out of scale with the children, and of more than heroic proportions. When I asked about this, Irmã Dores affirmed that the proportions were natural. It is my memory that she added the impression of our Lady appearing taller than average height, but I cannot state this with certainty. Later on, she did approve this feature of the new statue, however.

Of course, there was much of the interview that I failed to record. Irmã Dores often spoke rapidly, and long intervals of conversation sometimes went by without being translated. Frequently I broke in and pleaded for pause and interpretation, dreading to lose even a little of what was said. But the substance of all was conveyed to me. When I would scold the three Portuguese speakers for forgetting me, Irmã Dores would smile and stop; then I would catch up on my notes.

Perhaps I was too much occupied with what was wrong about my statue to write down Irmã Dores's favorable comments. I remembered them later at the hotel. I had asked her if the statue seemed to be light, that is, without weight (I had made this quite an objective in modeling it). She answered, "Yes. It gives the idea of lightness better than the others."

Begging, I must admit, for some further expression of approval, I held the figure in different positions for her renewed inspection. She said that the face on my statue seemed too old.

"Seen from the side it is better," she said. That was consoling, but hardly a quotable recommendation.

Retained from the first figure is the slightly inclined position of our Lady. When I asked Irmã Dores if our Lady bent forward, she said, "Yes. Because we were all small, below her feet."

The hour was now late. The friendly attitude of both Mother Provincial and Irmã Dores encouraged me to ask if we might return to inquire about the contents of the message of Fatima. Mother Provincial readily assented, and we took our leave.

I left the little statue in the parlor with some faint, fading hope that Irmã Dores might come in my absence and look again, and see the charm that I had tried, I thought successfully, to place in it.

8

THE MESSAGE OF FATIMA

Oporto, to which we returned that evening, was stirring with activity. The crowded impression I had gotten of the city when I first saw it from the train was confirmed in our walk down a shop-filled street to the central square, the Praça da Liberdade. There it seemed as if the entire population had poured down the twisting, cobbled streets with the rain and had filled cafés, sidewalks, stores, and rows of yellow streetcars. Automobile horns in Oporto seemed even more excited and persistent than those of Lisbon. It was a strange setting for reflection on our visit with Irmã Dores.

Interesting as that visit had been, it had not turned out quite according to plan. Irmã Dores had liked the profile of the statue and the attitude of the figure, but everything else needed correction. The drawings I had planned for minor corrections would have to carry an entirely new design. I wished I had the conveniences necessary for modeling a new statue. It would have been provident to have brought clay and tools for such a job, but I had not considered that my statue might be so far away from the reality of the vision.

After dinner, at Father Gardiner's invitation, Mr. Ronald Symington came to the hotel. Deeply devoted to Our Lady of Fatima, he had assisted the sick at the pilgrimages in the Cova da Iria for years in the capacity of stretcher-bearer. He was most interested in the details of our visit. Father Gardiner spoke with admiration of Irmã Dores. He declared that our Lady could not have chosen a better witness, so clear and simple had her answers been, and so sure and solid her personality.

I asked Mr. Symington about miracles at Fatima. He told me that he had been very close to Maria da Silva when she was cured. She was the one whom Father Gardiner had also seen. Mr. Symington declared that she had been "absolutely moribund" and that she arose as the Blessed Sacrament passed.

Then he spoke of a woman whom he had helped carry to the place of the sick on the same day. Her people apologized for her not thanking him and explained that she was mute. As the statue of our Lady passed by her, she joined the crowd in singing a hymn. Mr. Symington hastened to add, "Of course, this would not be a miracle from the medical point of view." He said that on that day, May 13, 1946, the crowd was estimated at 700,000. "The general Communion was a most astonishing sight; it went on, and on, and on; 130,000 went to Holy Communion."

Mr. Symington solved part of my problem about the statue by offering me the hospitality of his home, where, he said, I would have space to work on a new statue, if I so desired. I would have to find materials and make adjustments in my plans; but a new statue seemed to be the only means of fulfilling the purpose for which I had come to Portugal. I decided to remain.

We met with Irmã Dores and Mother Corte Real again in the morning. I told Mother Provincial that I had decided to make a new statue.

"Father, why don't you stay here and make it?" she said.

I felt like answering, "Mother, why don't I?" but told her instead that I thought the arrangement would be very nice; and I gratefully accepted.

She assured me there was plenty of room; the entire priest's house was unoccupied. But space was a minor consideration at this point. I would have been content with a lean-to for the work in order to have the privilege of making the statue right there.

Irmã Dores was waiting patiently for the questioning. She seemed more at ease than she had been the day before. I was going to ask her about the contents of the revelations made to her by our Lady, and I wanted to make clear to her my reverence in approaching the subject.

"Although I have an infinite curiosity, as everyone has, about the revelations made to her," I said to Mother Provincial, "I wish you would tell Sister that I will not ask any question that I do not see related to the welfare of souls."

Mother Provincial replied: "Irmã Dores knows that already; she is very keen."

Interpretations of the message of Fatima are many and varied. Generally, certain basic ideas are found in all of them: penance, sacrifice, the Rosary, devotion to the Immaculate Heart, the punitive character of war, the hopes for peace and for the conversion of

Russia. Different authors had given emphasis to different points. Now I wished to have these ideas clarified and correlated by the person through whom they had been given to the world at Fatima.

First in importance was the general motivation of the apparitions. I asked Irmã Dores to put this motivation into words.

"The conversion of sinners, and the return of souls to God," she said. "This idea was repeated in all the apparitions; that is why I consider it the principal message."

"Would you give a quotation of our Lady that expresses this motivation?" I asked.

She replied, "In October, our Lady said: 'Do not offend our Lord anymore; He is already much offended.'"

"Did our Lady address this to you three children or to the whole world?" I asked.

"I believe it was for the whole world."

In every apparition the Blessed Virgin had asked the children to make sacrifices, both to appease divine justice and to bring about the conversion of sinners. They had responded with heroic penance and patience. Was such extraordinary self-sacrifice requested of everyone? Recently Irmã Dores had been reported to have said that the sacrifice asked for by Our Lady of Fatima was merely that sacrifice necessary for the fulfillment of duty.

"When our Lady asked for sacrifice, did she ask merely for the observance of the commandments?"

Irmã Dores answered: "The meaning we took was that she wanted voluntary sacrifices—of course, after keeping the commandments, because, if we started making voluntary sacrifices without keeping the commandments, it wouldn't be much good."

She went on to warn me, however, not to confuse what she had just said with the wish expressed by our Lady in 1940. It was quite easy for me to avoid such confusion, for I knew nothing of

1940. Irmã Dores explained that in 1917 our Lady had asked for penance and sacrifice and that the children had understood this to mean voluntary sacrifice, but that "in 1940 she asked again for penance and sacrifice but the penance and sacrifice necessary for fulfilling religious duties and the duties of one's state."

I inquired if this was a mitigation of our Lady's earlier request. Irmã Dores's reply was typical of her factual reporting, free of the elaborations of her own opinion: "Our Lady did not explain that to me."

Mother Corte Real reminded us that the children of Fatima were "children of the mountains" and could hardly be expected to understand such theological distinctions.

Looking back later on the situation, I wondered how it all must have appeared to Irmã Dores and to Mother Provincial. The interrogation by two white-robed friars, their seriousness and note-taking might have been faintly suggestive of the Inquisition, although the seriousness was really begotten of reverence. We were there as disciples, not masters. But whatever the appearances, Irmã Dores was fully capable of coping with us. She was not troubled by any crackling of faggots. Nor was there confirmation of the possibility suggested by Mother Provincial that the children did not clearly understand the nature of the sacrifice requested by our Lady in 1917.

"Obviously she wanted more than the fulfillment of duty," Irmã Dores replied to an interpretation offered by Mother Provincial, "because she had already asked us not to offend God—that means doing one's duty—then she went on to ask for sacrifice and penance."

Mother Corte Real ventured a further explanation, the content of which escaped me, to which Irmã Dores replied with an emphatic finality that terminated the discussion of sacrifice:

"But they don't do their duty! If they did, our Lord would be more content."

"What were the devotions recommended by Our Lady at Fatima?" I asked.

"The Rosary and Communions of reparation," she replied.

For Rosary, Irmã Dores used the word *Terço*, the Portuguese name for the five-decade Rosary.

"In all the apparitions our Lady mentioned the Rosary (*Terço*); in the third apparition she said she would come to ask for Communions of reparation."

She went on to say that the concrete request for the devotion of the Communions of reparation of the Five First Saturdays came later, mentioning 1926. Then she gave the conditions of the devotion indicated by our Lady. "She asked for Communions of reparation, Confession, a quarter-hour meditation on the mysteries of the Rosary, and the *Terço*."

In a letter I received on my return to the United States replying to an inquiry I had made after the interviews, Irmã Dores mentioned the triple demand of our Lady for this devotion: "In 1925, 1926, and 1927, request and insistence on the Communions of reparation of the Five First Saturdays." Her mention of 1926 in the interview must have had to do with the detailing of all the conditions, for it was in that apparition that our Lady clarified the initial revelation of the devotion, which she had made in 1925.

"Did our Lady mention the First Saturdays in 1917?" I asked.

"She said: 'I shall come back to ask for the consecration of Russia and Communions of reparation.'" She remarked that Father De Marchi's first edition was correct on this quotation.

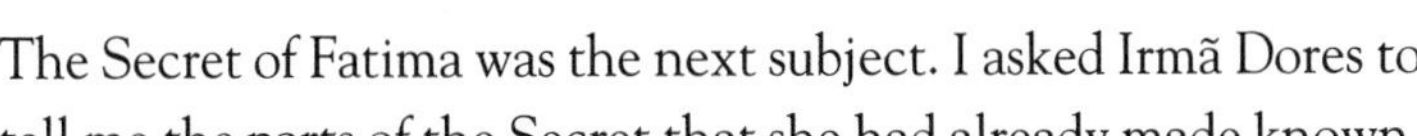

The Secret of Fatima was the next subject. I asked Irmã Dores to tell me the parts of the Secret that she had already made known.

She answered: "The parts of the Secret already revealed are the vision of hell; and that she would come back to ask for the consecration of Russia and for Communions of reparation."

The consecration of Russia and the Communions of reparation are the two forms of homage to the Immaculate Heart that were requested at Fatima.

Irmã Dores stated that the book *Jacinta*, by Father Galamba, exactly reported the revealed portions of the Secret.

"What it has is correct; but it hasn't all," she said.

"Can any more you have written about be published?" I asked.

"No. I can't publish anything," she said, laughing. She made it clear by a simple reference to the authority of the bishop, that the measure and manner of her presenting the message of our Lady to the world are dictated entirely by obedience.

Belief in the message of Fatima depends on the credibility of Irmã Dores as the only witness of the message in its entirety. By making known her communication, ecclesiastical authority has implicitly assured us of her reliability. It is further confirmed in this evidence of her complete submission to authority. She speaks of Fatima only to her ecclesiastical superiors or with their permission; her testimony is simple and without personal commentary.

We inquired further about her writings, which we had called her memoirs, and the published parts of which, the bishop had said, were contained in the book *Jacinta*. We wondered if these writings of Irmã Dores were limited to the memoirs referred to by the bishop. Father Gardiner inquired why her writings could not be published in their entirety. Irmã Dores answered: "They must contain private things that the bishop thinks inconvenient to publish; and they might contain things about Russia that the bishop thinks should not be published." She added that it would be unwise to publish all her notes because of living persons referred to in them.

I returned to the actual wording of the Secret. In order to have this central passage of the revelations of Fatima accurate I asked Father Gardiner to read, phrase by phrase, a printed text that I had, for her approval or correction. The following is the complete text, as corrected:

> You have just seen hell, where the souls of poor sinners go. To save them the Lord wishes to establish in the world devotion to my Immaculate Heart. If people do what I shall tell you, many souls will be saved and there will be peace.
>
> The war will soon end. But if men do not stop offending the Lord it will not be long before another and worse one begins; that will be in the Pontificate of Pius XI.
>
> When you see the night illuminated by an unknown light, know that it is the great sign which God is giving you, indicating that the world, on account of its innumerable crimes, will soon be punished by war, famine, and persecutions against the Church and the Holy Father.
>
> In order to prevent it I shall come to ask for the consecration of Russia to my Immaculate Heart, as well as Communions of reparation on the First Saturdays of the month.
>
> If my requests are granted Russia will be converted and there will be peace. Otherwise Russia will spread her errors through the world fomenting wars and persecutions against the Church. Many will be martyred, the Holy

> Father will have much to suffer; several nations will be destroyed.
>
> In the end my Immaculate Heart will triumph. The Holy Father will consecrate Russia to me, Russia will be converted, and there will be a certain period of peace.

The English text had had the expression, "in the next Pontificate." Irmã Dores corrected it to read "in the Pontificate of Piux XI."

"In order to stop it I shall come to ask for the consecration of Russia to my Immaculate Heart" was the corrected version of the sentence that had read: "In order to stop it, I ask for the consecration of the world." Irmã Dores was emphatic in making the correction about Russia. "No!" she said, "not the world! Russia! Russia!"

The final sentence was supplied entirely by her.

In his address to the Portuguese nation on the silver jubilee of the apparitions, on October 31, 1942, Pope Pius XII had consecrated the world to the Immaculate Heart and had made special, descriptive mention of Russia. Some had regarded this as fulfillment of the request of our Lady. Others had stated that it was not sufficient, that all the bishops of the world were expected to join with the Holy Father in making the consecration of Russia.

"Did the Holy Father consecrate Russia to the Immaculate Heart?" I asked Irmã Dores.

"He included Russia in the consecration," she said. Then, very humbly, as if wishing that she were wrong, she added, "In the official way that our Lady asked for it? I don't think so."

Father Gardiner, wishing to make certain of this point, reframed the question, "Do you think that our Lady's request has been complied with?"

Irmã Dores replied: "As our Lady made it, no." But she added, "Whether our Lady accepted the consecration made in 1942 as fulfilling her wish, I don't know."

9
THE NEW PROJECT

At his home in Santa Cruz do Bispo the sculptor Guilhermo Thedim (brother of José Thedim) was very pleasant when Mr. Symington introduced me. He showed us into his workshop, where two assistants were carving a reproduction of one of his designs. Mr. Symington laid my problem before him. I was going to make a little statue of Our Lady of Fatima at the Colégio do Sardão, and I wanted to inquire of him where I could get the necessary tools and materials.

First, he looked about and located a small stand with an iron rod in it, which happened to be just the right height for the statue I planned. (To solve the problem of carrying the new statue, I had intended to make it the same size as the old one so that it would fit in the same case.) Then he gave us the addresses of an art supply store where I could purchase modeling tools, and of another shop that handled sculptor's clay and plaster.

We saw a reproduction of his brother's famous Fatima statue. This one, however, was undecorated, and the warm red of the cedar wood seemed to increase its charm.

We discussed Irmã Dores. Senhor Thedim was aware of her corrections. He showed us a statue that he had recently designed in conformity with those corrections. Although the design had only the two garments described by Irmã Dores and only the two decorative elements — the star and the pendant of light — the sleeves were quite full; the mantle was wide and flowing, and the figure was standing on a cloud.

Wishing to share with Senhor Thedim the information I had just gained from Irmã Dores, I pointed out that she had said that the sleeves appeared to be narrow, that the drapery fell very straight, and that there was no cloud. He felt that these details were a matter of necessary artistic interpretation.

Senhor Thedim's genuinely gracious manner relieved my uneasiness about being a foreign and rival sculptor in the field of Fatima. Perhaps he realized that the enviable opportunity I was to have of working under the guidance of Irmã Dores was probably made possible by the fact that I was a priest as well as a sculptor.

Father Gardiner decided to remain with the Symingtons while I stayed at the Colégio. He would visit occasionally, particularly on Monday, for the third interview; but the burden of his work as interpreter was finished, and there were others, in the community itself, notably Mother King, who could assist me by interpreting during the making of the statue.

I had expected to spend a rather solitary week at Sardão because of my ignorance of Portuguese, but, after the second interview with Irmã Dores, Mother Provincial introduced an Irish nun of the community, one of the teaching sisters, Mother Mary King, who had entered the order in Tui, Spain, in 1925 and had known Irmã Dores in the novitiate. I have since been most grateful for the roving instincts of the Irish, for Mother King's friendly aid and interpretation were the principal means of my association with Irmã Dores.

It was late by the time we reached Sardão. Mother King and two lay sisters who had waited up made light of the inconvenience we had caused them. The sisters quickly seized my luggage against my protest. Greetings and farewells had to be abbreviated because of a light rain. Father Gardiner and Mr. Symington said good night and wished me well. Then the great iron plates of the gate slammed shut, locking out the world and all that had gone before.

As the three nuns led the way through corridors and doorways out into the yard and toward the priest's house, I reflected on the strangeness of the immediate situation and wondered about the statue to be made, about Irmã Dores, and about the future, which, I felt, this little journey would somehow determine.

The apartment that was to be my home and workshop for the coming nine days was on the second floor of a boxlike building. To the right of the landing at the head of the staircase was a spacious parlor with tall windows on two sides. A divan, a plain table, and a few chairs were all the furnishings and could easily be moved about to allow for the work. Flooring throughout the apartment was of plain boards and had the appearance of being well scrubbed. Living quarters were on the left—a small office and a small bedroom, old-fashioned and simply furnished, but very neat and comfortable looking.

I went down to the door with the sisters and Mother King after depositing the bag and briefcase. As they were about to leave, a great clap of thunder accompanied by a cloudburst broke upon the house. One of the sisters ran for the main building, but Mother King, terrified of lightning, and Irmã Assunção, who may have been terrified but could not say so in English, remained. I was glad to have my solitary confinement postponed for the fifteen minutes that they had to wait until the storm abated.

The morning began with Mass in the chapel of the school. The high altar was undergoing repairs, and the chaplain was saying Mass at the Sacred Heart altar in the body of the chapel, beyond the Communion rail, when I arrived in the sacristy. While he distributed Holy Communion I held the plate. There was nothing singular about Irmã Dores as she received Communion; she showed only the ordinary seriousness and recollection of any devout communicant. This trait of being ordinary impressed me throughout my visit with her as a leading quality of her personality. The extraordinary graces that have been given to her are guarded and hidden by a very simple outward demeanor. Later, I chanced to see her in a hallway, carrying a dishpan into the kitchen. Her head erect, her steps brisk, she moved along with the same grace of plainness and habitude.

Mother Provincial arranged to have Mother King and two pupils of the school, the Barros-Gomes sisters, accompany me to Oporto on my tour of shopping for the tools, clay, and plaster that were the remaining requisites for the work. The girls, whose mother was English, were blonde and very British in appearance and accent. We went first to the parlor of the school. I wanted to get my statue, and Mother King wanted the girls to see it. So far as I know, Irmã Dores had not noticed or commented on it again. But the Barros-Gomes girls thought that the statue was "awfully nice!" (Before I left Vila Nova de Gaia, Mr. Symington kindly shipped the statue back to the United States for me; and, at this writing, the crate has not been opened.)

On the first morning of what I had expected to be Portuguese isolation it was odd to be riding in a taxi through the cities of Vila Nova de Gaia and Oporto with so much cheery British and Irish chatter in my ears. At a stationery and art supply store we found the modeling tools I needed. We hurried then to a remote corner of the city to reach the other shop before the noon closing time. With about fifty pounds of clay, wrapped in papers, and about a hundred pounds of plaster in a paper sack, safely in the trunk of the taxi, our mission was accomplished.

Just over the bridge in Vila Nova de Gaia we chanced to meet the car belonging to the Colégio; and into it we transferred our persons and our purchases. Mother King had not let me pay for the tools, and now she would not permit me to pay the taxi driver. Mother Provincial, she told me, had insisted on taking care of these expenses.

Back at the priest's house, I discovered that the clay was much too moist for immediate work on a small statue. I rolled out strips for drying, then arranged the chairs and table for the work. By placing the case for the statue on end, on the top of the table, I had a stand that, though rather insecure, was the right height for modeling. I then spread out the dozen or so small modeling tools on the newspaper that covered the table. Everything was now in readiness.

At lunch I had my first conversation in Portuguese, unassisted by an interpreter. The sister who served my meals in a small dining room on the ground floor of the Colégio was the young lay sister who had been with Mother King the night before, Irmã Assunção. She thought it fun to speak to me in Portuguese, pretending that I understood, yet knowing very well that I did not. I would reply in sentences of English, quite unintelligible to her, and win from her the most delightful laughter.

Despite the fact that I had heard the word Irmã used of Irmã Dores, I had been so preoccupied with the contents of the interviews and with her personality that I had not yet given attention to the meaning of her name. I did not know until this lunchtime that *Irmã* meant "Sister." Using pantomime, including the action of writing, and saying the word for "name" every way that I knew how, I managed to make my waitress understand the question "What is your name?"

"Irmã Assunção," she said.

Then she went into an amusing performance, which I later discovered was an explanation of the distinction between the nuns of the community who teach and those who are called lay sisters. The first are identified as Madre, or Mother; and the latter as Irmã, or Sister. The explanation consisted of the actions of mopping, scrubbing, washing and drying dishes, and cleaning and ironing clothes.

Father Gardiner came in about this time. I said to him, "We have just been having a conversation. I got as far as finding out that the sister serving me is named Sister Irmã Assunção." The discovery is one that Father Gardiner will probably never get over, for, afterward, in our visits with people who spoke Portuguese, he always enjoyed recounting the incident at Sardão when I found out that the name of my waitress was "Sister Irmã."

After lunch I began work on the statue, despite the softness of the clay. Mother King and Father Gardiner had come to witness the start of the work. But I could do little more than place a mass of clay on the iron bar, until the clay became firmer. It was quite formless, and both members of my audience expressed their wonder that anything could come of it. In fact, annoyed with the condition of the clay, and anxious about the task ahead, I wondered with them.

I spent all day Sunday in the studio alone trying to work the clay into condition and get sufficient modeling done so that Irmã Dores would have something to criticize on Monday. By the end of the day a figure was roughly shaped with arms in the position of the Blessed Virgin in the June apparition as I remembered Irmã Dores showing it to me.

When she came, in the morning, Irmã Dores brought with her a printed photo of Senhor José Thedim's statue. A little hair showed over the forehead beneath the mantle. Perhaps, she let me understand, it would not hurt to do something like this about the hair. She was inclined to make the concession because of my insistence on the point during the first interview. I told her that the detail had ceased to be a problem for me and that my only interest now was to make a statue that would resemble the apparition as closely as possible in every respect.

Mother Provincial and Mother King accompanied Irmã Dores. They remained seated, while Irmã Dores stood beside me to observe the modeling from close range.

I had expected that she would be there for only a few minutes, make what comments were necessary, and leave. But after half an hour there was still no sign that she intended to go. This was all to my liking, but I had to be more comfortable for the work. I removed my Roman collar and replaced it with a scarf; then I asked to smoke.

Irmã Dores limited her first criticism to the positions of the arms. With meticulous precision she corrected both the height and angle of each forearm and the gesture of each hand. She would assume these positions, by way of explaining. She would study especially the angle of the right hand, as if recalling the hand of our Lady and the projection of light that came from it upon her when she was a child. Knotting her brows slightly, she would draw an imaginary line from her hand downward, as if from our Lady's hand to the children.

When the session terminated, the general proportions of the figure and the positions of the hands had been established. Work on details would have to wait until the next morning because the afternoon would be devoted to another interrogation on the revelations of Fatima.

10

PARTICULAR PROBLEMS

The chance to discuss with Irmã Dores more than the physical details of the apparitions had come as an agreeable surprise. Many more interviews might have been granted, had I requested them; but I believed it prudent to limit my demands on the kindness of Irmã Dores and Mother Provincial, both to spare them the tedium that these discussions entailed and to allow more time for the work that was my specific objective, the modeling of the statue.

For this final interrogation I had tried to prepare questions that would cover all the remaining problems I had heard raised about Fatima, and all that had occurred to me.

"When our Lady said in 1917 that another and a worse war would begin in the next Pontificate, did she use the words, 'in the Pontificate of Pius XI'?"

Irmã Dores: "Yes, 'Pius XI.' "

"The 'great light' that our Lady spoke of: was it (as reported) the Aurora Borealis of January 25–26, 1938?"

"Yes."

"What event, then, was considered the beginning of the war? Actual hostilities began with the invasion of Poland in September 1939, Pius XII then being Pope."

"For me the invasion of Austria was the beginning of the war. The Pope proclaimed it as such."

"Would the consecration of Russia to the Immaculate Heart have prevented the last war?"

"According to the promise of our Lady, if they had made it, I think so."

"In 1927, it is said, our Lord spoke to you from the tabernacle, giving you permission to write all that our Lady had revealed concerning devotion to the Immaculate Heart. Did this not include the consecration of Russia?"

"I think so. I wrote of it in 1929."

"Was this wish made known to the Holy Father at that time?"

"I told my confessor; he informed the bishop of Leiria. After a while my confessor said that the communication had been sent to the Holy Father."

"It seems from the words of our Lady in 1917 that the war of 1939–1945 was threatened as punishment for sin. But the warning was not known generally until 1942, after the punishment had begun. How is this explained?"

"This had all been said in 1917, that is, that men must amend their lives, that they must not offend God, that He was already much offended."

She explained that our Lady had told her in 1917 that this part of the Secret was not to be revealed until 1927. The threat of punishment was part of the Secret.

Asked if the bishop had told her not to publish this, she replied, "He didn't tell me anything. He did not publish it. After all, this was not for the bishop to publish since the communication had been made to the Pope. The part necessary for the people to know was already known since 1917."

"Can you give an explanation of why the portions of the Secret now revealed had to remain secret? They seem to include doctrines always known: that sinners are punished eternally in hell, and that through the intercession of our Lady sinners can be saved. The only thing not known is the wish of our Lady that Russia be consecrated to her Immaculate Heart."

"I explain this by saying that that is what our Lady wanted. The bishop says it was providential, because it did more good at the time it was revealed."

"You are quoted as having said that our Lady wishes all the bishops of the world to join with the Pope on a special day in consecrating Russia to her Immaculate Heart. Is this true?"

"Our Lady commanded that the Holy Father consecrate Russia to her Immaculate Heart and that he command all the bishops to do it also in union with him at the same time."

"May I inquire when our Lady made this known?"

"In 1929."

I then expressed surprise, noting that it had never been published before, to my knowledge (that is, the condition of co-consecration by all the bishops), and that the cardinal said he had never heard of it.

Commenting on the cardinal's statement, Irmã Dores said that he must have forgotten, "for he saw the draft of my letter to the Pope."

She then went out to get the letter. It was a careful draft in a school copybook. Father Gardiner and I read it, her intention being simply that we verify the condition. It was most clearly expressed. The letter was addressed to the present Holy Father.

"Is the promise that Russia will be converted conditional or absolute?"

"In the end [i.e., of the text of July 13], absolute."

"I would like you to state the importance of the Rosary in the message of our Lady."

"My impression is that the Rosary is of greatest value not only according to the words of Our Lady at Fatima but according to the effects of the Rosary one sees throughout history. My impression is that our Lady wanted to give ordinary people who might not know how to pray this simple method of getting closer to God."

"Did our Lady ask for the Family Rosary?"

"Not expressly." Irmã Dores added a word of commendation for this devotion.

"Does our Lady request that every Catholic recite the Rosary every day?"

Keeping the record straight, Irmã Dores's reply dealt first with the restriction "Catholic."

"She didn't express anyone in particular, but everyone in general." She then quoted our Lady as having said, "Say the Rosary always." The word our Lady used for "Rosary," Irmã Dores explained, was *Terço* (the five-decade beads). She commented that our Lady always used the word *Terço* until October, the last day, when she said, "I am the Lady of the Rosary" (or *Rosário*).

"Did Our Lady use these words: 'Say the Rosary every day and say it well (or devoutly)'?"

"No. She may have said 'every day' in some apparition—she definitely said 'always'" (Portuguese, *sempre*).

"Did our Lady indicate any intentions for which the Rosary should be said?"

"In the first apparition she said only, 'Say the Rosary always'; in the last apparition she said, 'Say the Rosary for the end of the war.'"

"Was devotion to Our Lady of Mount Carmel recommended?"

"In the fourth apparition at Valinhos, she said that Our Lady of Mount Carmel, Our Lady of Sorrows, Saint Joseph and the infant Jesus would come to bless the world." Irmã Dores then hesitated and expressed uncertainty of the date of this promise, that is, whether it was made during the August or September apparition.

"Did our Lady say anything about the scapular?"

"No."

"Was devotion to Our Lady of Sorrows recommended?"

"No."

I happened to think of a question, not in logical order, but I wanted the answer and asked it here lest I forgot: "When did you ask our Lady for a miracle?"

Irmã Dores replied that she made the petition in either July or August; she was uncertain which.

"Did you then make the promise known immediately to the people?"

"Yes."

"Would you consider the consecration of individuals, dioceses, and countries to the Immaculate Heart a fitting expression of devotion to the Immaculate Heart?"

"Such consecrations were not expressly requested, but I think they would be pleasing to our Lady and would bring special graces on dioceses and nations."

The angel who appeared to the children in 1916 taught them two prayers. Our Lady taught them two more during the July apparition in 1917. One was to be said after each decade of the Rosary.

Nearly every book on Fatima seemed to have a version of these prayers that differed from the next. There was a frequently printed error of translation in the prayer after the decades, which made the petition seem to be a plea for the souls in Purgatory. I discussed this matter with Mother Corte Real. She said that Irmã Dores's understanding of the phrase in question—"especially those in greatest need" (*principalmente as que mais precisarem*)—was "those in imminent danger of damnation."

I asked Irmã Dores if she would write out all four prayers for me. She agreed to do so.

Next, I wished to clear up points in the appearance of our Lady that were not certain from my first interview. "How old did our Lady appear to be?"

Irmã Dores smiled at the question. "Perhaps seventeen." The smile was not explained but I took it to mean that this inquiry was not new to her and that it could hardly be answered exactly without her having asked the question of our Lady.

"Did she always appear the same age?"

"Yes."

"Was she always sad?"

"She never smiled. She was pleasant but sad."

"What do you say of her beauty?"

"There are no words to express her beauty."

"What do you say of her kindness?" I was obviously trying to get a statement to quote. Irmã Dores discerned the device, no doubt, and expressed her displeasure with a reproving sort of laughter.

She turned to Mother Provincial and made a remark that was punctuated by the same laughter.

"What did she say?" I asked Father Gardiner.

"She said she thinks these questions are foolish," Father Gardiner answered, very much amused. I pleaded that we who were not privileged to see our Lady want to know all we can about her. But Irmã Dores simply replied, "Nothing can be said."

"Do you recall the number of points on the star?"

"I don't know."

"Was there only one star?"

"Yes."

"Was the yellow light all around the bottom of the mantle?"

"It is my impression that it was all around. The intensity of this light seemed to be a reflection of the light from within."

"You say that in May and July she opened her hands in a gesture like the *Dominus vobiscum*. In May this expressed satisfaction with your agreeing to make sacrifice. What occasioned this gesture in July?"

Irmã Dores answered that at the gesture a ray of light came from the apparition and penetrated their hearts. "Was there the wound of a sword, or a sword, in the Immaculate Heart?"

"No."

I asked her to give an account of the series of apparitions in October.

Irmã Dores said that at first our Lady appeared as usual and that at a certain point she turned her hand toward the sun. Irmã Dores said that apparently at this moment she made the exclamation "Look at the sun," which she does not remember making. "Then appeared at her side, first, Saint Joseph and the Child Jesus; then our Lord; then there were changes of light in which our Lady took on different aspects—Our Lady of Sorrows and

Our Lady of Mount Carmel. While this was going on, the people cried out that they saw the phenomenon in the sun; I myself did not see it."

I asked if she took note of the details of this series of apparitions sufficiently to be able to describe them to me so that I might make sketches of them.

She answered: "The changes that took place were all changes of light; I can't explain."

Then followed a series of miscellaneous questions.

"During the apparitions, were you aware of any of the things mentioned by others, such as the shower of flowers, colors in the sky?"

"No." She remarked that others saw a cloud.

"Did others speak to you of these things? If so, of what?"

"Many people spoke to me of the sun, but I wanted to get away." She added the interesting observation that not all seemed to have seen the same things.

"When the bishop made his first visit to Fatima, he saw a shower like rose petals; then he believed," she said.

"Did the apparition strain your eyes?" (I had read conflicting reports.)

"It didn't really hurt the eyes, but it was a very intense light, and one felt some difference. Our eyesight was not powerful enough."

"Have you any recollection of the numbers present at the various apparitions?" (I explained that there were wide differences in the estimates of numbers.)

"In June there was only a group, not a crowd; at the other apparitions the whole place was full of people, lined up from the Cova to Aljustrel. From the third apparition on, there were tremendous crowds. It was hard to make one's way through them."

"Jacinta is reported to have said of those who would die in war that nearly all of them would be lost. Did our Lady say this?"

"I don't remember her [Jacinta's] saying this. Our Lady never said anything about those dying in war going to hell." Irmã Dores then offered what she believed to be the origin of the mistaken quotation: "I don't know whether it was through revelation or intuition, but Jacinta had visions of people dead in the streets from war. Jacinta in horror said: 'Can it be that most of these will go to hell?' This was her own [Jacinta's] reflection."

"Did our Lady say a certain Amelia would be in purgatory until the end of the world?"

"True."

"How old was Amelia?"

"Eighteen."

When I stated that this troubled many people, Irmã Dores replied that she did not think it very remarkable, since one could go to hell for all eternity for missing Mass on Sunday.

She had answered the last question on my list. We thanked her and Mother Provincial for their patience and kindness and said that we had enjoyed the interviews very much. Mother Provincial very sweetly assured us that it was a pleasure to have assisted us in the work of Our Lady of Fatima.

At a signal from Mother Corte Real, Irmã Dores left to get tea. She returned in a little while with a tray that had, besides tea, several kinds of cakes and breads and sweet spreads for them. I protested that I was being overfed by the sisters. Father Gardiner added that after being so well treated at Sardão, I would be unable to get back to the rigors of community life.

Irmã Dores was pouring our tea. There was a smile on her face that did not conceal her seriousness as she commented: "It will do him no harm. When he goes back, he can make sacrifice."

11

OUR STATUE

The modeling of the statue began on Saturday afternoon, February 8, and was completed at noon on Friday, the fourteenth.

Irmã Dores first came to criticize on Monday morning. She returned on Tuesday and stayed many hours, morning and afternoon, and, thereafter, every morning and afternoon until the work was done. Mother Provincial and Mother King were sometimes with her but nearly always there was her great friend and confidant, the woman who was her superior for many years at the convent in Spain, Mother Cunha-Mattos, known in the community as Mother Superior.

In a situation evidently all to her liking, Irmã Dores became relaxed. When she was not standing beside me dictating and criticizing she would sit with Mother Cunha-Mattos and talk in a gay manner, just as if I had never been a stranger.

There were several reasons for this change of Irmã Dores's attitude. She was not now under the stress of being questioned but rather in a position of giving orders in a project very close to her heart, for which she seemed confident of final success.

There were pleasantries exchanged, also, which helped to dissolve strangeness, notably the general amusement at my attire. Because of the severe cold I usually wore a sweater with my street suit and a white muffler around my neck. Then I had, pinned to the lapels of my coat, a light-blue denim apron lent to me by one of the lay sisters. Sometimes when it was not too cold I would wear the habit with this apron pinned on the capuche.

Mother Superior, in her imperfect English, liked to joke about my chain-smoking, in a manner of half serious reproof that I blandly ignored. I defended the addiction as a harmless kind of fidgeting that relieved tension.

"What does this mean—'fidgeting'?" Mother Superior asked.

I explained by giving examples of thumb-twiddling, paper tearing, and nail-biting. "Nearly everyone fidgets," I said.

Now that she understood, Mother Superior pursued her point: "But I don't smoke; and I don't fidgets."

Irmã Dores herself expressed, on several occasions, in different words, the most important reason for her enjoyment of the work. She had always wanted to see a statue of this apparition of the Immaculate Heart. She had wished many times that she could be a sculptor so as to be able to make it herself, but, since she was not, she said, she believed that God had sent me to make this statue.

Sometimes Mother King was present to interpret. On one such occasion Irmã Dores had been silent for a long time, busy making a rosary. Suddenly she looked up from her work and said, "You know, when you two speak English, it sounds as though you were not articulating at all."

Mother King told her that she should learn English; then she began a lesson. Irmã Dores struggled to imitate the sound, "Our Lady." Something like "hour laddy" was the result. She thought it was a very odd way to say *nossa Senhora.* Then Mother King tested her with "coffee" and "tea." These she repeated pretty well.

"Say, 'okay,'" I demanded.

She made a brave attempt that ended in "ho-kayee." Then she asked what it meant. Mother King explained, then laughingly scolded me: "Aren't you ashamed, teaching Irmã Dores slang!"

The rosary that Irmã Dores was working on was intended for the statue, a tiny chaplet of mother-of-pearl beads, which she linked together with great skill and speed. She had the beads on a coil of fine silver wire that she twisted with pliers into hardly visible links as the rosary grew, bead by bead. She stopped the work frequently to examine the statue. The distraction may account for the fact that one of the decades has only nine beads.

I asked Irmã Dores about the size of the beads carried by our Lady. She took hold of a bead of Mother King's rosary and said they were about that size. The little beads of the rosary she was making were therefore in good scale. Irmã Dores could not say definitely that the rosary carried by our Lady was of five decades, rather than fifteen. But she did assert that the Rosary extended about to the knees when our Lady's right hand was in the position of the June apparition. From this information and Irmã Dores's identification of the size of the beads, it is a fair deduction that our Lady's rosary must have been of five decades, for one of fifteen decades with that size bead would have gone far below her feet.

Irmã Dores said that the rosary was all white, the cross included. She apologized for having to put on the rosary she was making a cross that was aluminum and a bit oversize. She explained that she had no other.

For most of the work, interpretation was not needed; a basic vocabulary of about a dozen words sufficed along with Irmã

Dores's gestures for me to understand "higher," "lower," "left," "right," "larger," "smaller," and so on.

Irmã Dores spent much of the time on her feet at the statue, watching the modeling closely and interrupting it often for corrections. These she would make at times by actually touching the clay either with her fingers or a modeling tool, a deed that performed by anyone else would have incurred my wrath. But I was now by choice her instrument in making a statue, the object of which was to be an entirely documentary portrayal of the apparition of June 13, 1917. I had set aside all particular preferences and prejudices in favor of doing everything exactly as she wished it to be done.

For instance, I had modeled the veil after her description as closely as possible to the head and neck, filling in the corners that would naturally be created by a light material falling from the head. I was avoiding undesirable "undercutting," which causes deep shadows. But Irmã Dores insisted that the veil be moved out more from the head. When I moved it out slightly she demanded that it be moved more. A little more, and she asked for still more, until finally she made her intentions clear by actually modeling part of the veil herself. The little curve that she made to the right of the face was the only modeling that she did on the statue. It still remains in the figure and has been reproduced in the larger one.

There was not a detail of the execution that Irmã Dores missed or on which she did not comment with either approval or correction.

Her first observations, and perhaps the most important of all because they qualified the entire design, concerned the treatment given to the drapery. Before starting the work, I had wondered how I might suggest the "waves of light" of which Irmã Dores had spoken during the interviews. She had said, "The light was in waves and gave the impression of a garment with folds."

Two things seemed to be important in interpreting this description: One was that, although there was a suggestion of folds, the folds could not be realistic; they should not appear to be actual folds of fabric, but rather in some manner to suggest folds. The second was that the folds should have the vibrant character of the light that she described. Therefore, in making the lines of the tunic as I drew the tool down for each line, I moved it from side to side rapidly with each downward stroke. The action resulted in a basically straight line that, however, was broken with slightly scooped and concave forms. I asked Irmã Dores if this treatment suggested the "waves of light." She said, "Yes, it does very well."

But she had a change to make. I had made the folds, or these waves, continuous lines, starting from the top of the tunic and ending at the hem. Irmã Dores insisted that they be broken at the waist, alternating, so that the ridges of the folds falling from the waist corresponded with the hollows of the folds above the waist. She explained that this resembled the apparition in that, while there was no sash or visible cord drawing the waist in, there definitely was a break of the form at the waist.

She made me add clay along the right side of the tunic, eliminating the curve that I had thought balanced well with the movement of the left leg. She insisted that the drapery should fall down very straight and that the underlying shape of the body should not be at all obvious. Nor could the folds reveal the form of the breasts more than by a slight curving of the bosom.

I had placed the "little ball of light" directly at the waist. Irmã Dores noticed this and made me raise it about a quarter of an inch to its present position. She also pointed precisely to the place where the "rays of sunlight" supporting the little ball of light entered into the corner of the veil. She determined the length and shape of the mantle or veil, indicating that on the right side it curved back and fell in a fold; on the left it fell straight and was a bit lower.

In order to clarify the appearance of the heart and thorns Irmã Dores went out into the garden and came back soon with branches of thorns. She joined the ends of one of them together to show how the thorns encircled the heart vertically and the approximate number that fastened into the heart. Incidentally, she said that of the entire apparition only the thorns were not made of light; they were simply burnt-out, brown, and natural in quality. She herself placed the heart surrounded by thorns in its right position after I had put it a little more than she wished toward center.

The modeling so interested Irmã Dores that she decided one day to try modeling herself. She brought along a bamboo stick about the length of the statue I was making. When I discovered her intentions, she laughed as if in admission of her presumption. I tried to encourage her and got for her some of the firmer clay out of the container, a washtub in the corner of the room.

After a while I noticed that she had the wire intended to support the shoulders fairly near to where the elbows would come. I warned her that she would have to move the wire higher if she wanted to fit the entire figure on the stick. She studied the problem a while, then changed her mind. She would make only the head and shoulders. I noticed her occasionally during the process, studying the statue I was making and trying to copy it.

A good while later she had succeeded in shaping the general form of a head in good proportions, covered, as was the head of the statue, with a veil. But she never went on to the features. When the session ended, she smiled and threw her unfinished work, bamboo stick and all, into the washtub.

In the beginning Irmã Dores marked the clay where the star was to go, near the bottom of the tunic. For some time I did not get around to the star but simply kept a little lump of clay there to show where it would eventually be modeled. Finally, tired of looking at the lump of clay in my travels around the surface, I decided to make a star.

I had asked Irmã Dores how many points there were in the star. Her answer was, "I don't know. Does it make any difference?" Then she inquired about the meaning of the different numbers of points on stars. Not an authority on this subject, I merely joked about it. I said, "Well, the Star of Bethlehem has five points; the Star of David, crossed triangles, has six; and if you want to bring in Saint Dominic, he has a star with eight points." She left the decision entirely up to me by saying, "I don't know."

Without consciously making a decision, I made a five-pointed star. It later occurred to me that this is the number of points in the Soviet star. A fitting symbol, I thought, of the conversion of Russia that the Blessed Virgin had prophesied: Russia will one day be an ornament at our Lady's feet. I proposed this interpretation to Irmã Dores and received the not surprising answer, "I don't know."

Until further revelation makes the meaning of these elements known, only conjecture can be offered for their symbolism. I wonder if possibly the pendant, as some people call it, the "little ball of light," hung from "two rays of sunlight," might not mean the victory of the Immaculate Heart of Mary over the world. The cord-like rays do make a V, and our Lady did declare, "In the end my Immaculate Heart will triumph." But if I offered this explanation to Irmã Dores, I am sure it would win from her exactly the same comment that she made about my interpretation of the star.

The face and hands of the figure were her chief concern and mine also. It was not too long before she became satisfied with the position of the hands and of the figure generally, but for a time I feared that the face would never satisfy her. Her criticisms were endless; she kept making me change now the forehead, now the cheeks, now the mouth, chin, and eyes. Mother Cunha-Mattos scolded her for being too particular. She warned that I would never finish the statue if she did not finish her criticisms. Irmã Dores's answer was, "I can't tell him I like it if I don't."

After a day that I devoted almost entirely to the modeling of the face, Mother King wondered if I would be hurt by her telling me what Irmã Dores had said. I assured her that I wanted to know. Then she quoted Irmã Dores as saying, "He has the position of the hands right but the face is not yet beautiful enough." This made me concentrate with almost furious activity on the alteration of the features for a possible improvement before Irmã Dores arrived. When she came, she expressed her feeling that the face was better. But this implied that it was not quite good enough.

"*Mais pequena, mais pequena!*" (smaller, smaller), she kept saying of the mouth. I kept obeying against my will until I thought the mouth too small. Then she studied it carefully, and I was afraid she was about to say smaller again when instead, and much worse, she said, "*Mais alta*" (higher). Well, one does not just raise up a mouth. That meant I had to make a new one. There were times like this when annoyance nearly took the place of reverence in my feelings, when I could forget that Irmã Dores was Lucy dos Santos of Fatima.

Mother Cunha-Mattos sympathized with my near desperation and told me not to worry too much about the criticisms that Irmã Dores made. She startled me by adding, "Your ideas of beauty may be just as good as hers." I hastened, with tones of an ultimatum, to have Mother King convey to Irmã Dores the following question:

"Are you basing your criticisms of the face upon your conception of what is beautiful or upon the apparition?"

Irmã Dores replied, "As far as I am able, I am trying to show you what I saw."

This gave me patience to carry on until at last Irmã Dores expressed her satisfaction and ceased firing corrections. I must admit that, although it is a face that I would never have made without her direction, I much prefer the face of this statue to that of the one that I first made.

Some of the sisters feared that I might have made the figure too tall and referred the question to Irmã Dores. She answered with an approval of the proportions. "Our Lady," she added, "was very graceful" *(muito graciosa)*.

At noon on Friday the work seemed far enough advanced for casting and, with Irmã Dores's consent, I decided to call the modeling finished.

I had wondered all along if I might be allowed to photograph Irmã Dores? Completion of the statue gave me the possibility, and the establishment of most cordial relations with the sisters gave me hope.

I explained to Mother Provincial that I wished to bring back with me to the United States a series of photographs for lecturing on Fatima and that it would be most helpful and interesting if I could include among them photographs of Irmã Dores. After a moment's consideration Mother Provincial decided favorably, on the condition that I would not make use of the photographs until and unless the bishop gave his consent.

Mother King conveyed to Irmã Dores the information that I was going to photograph her. At first Irmã Dores was somewhat disturbed, but when Mother King explained that it was the wish of Mother Provincial, she became not only agreeable but most cooperative. I selected a stand about four feet high from the apartment. Irmã Dores insisted upon carrying the statue herself.

I was a little afraid because, held at the bottom, the statue would exert great leverage on her wrists if its equilibrium was in the least disturbed. However, Irmã Dores's wrists were quite equal to the burden. Accompanied by several of the sisters, we went to the yard outside the Colégio to take the pictures.

I had mentally rehearsed this process often, had my lenses all prepared and the light reading taken for both still and motion-picture cameras. I worked with great haste but found that haste was unnecessary, for after I had taken several photographs of Irmã Dores standing beside the statue, both she and Mother King suggested a change of site to one farther out in the garden where there would be a more satisfactory background.

It occurred to Irmã Dores that it would be nice to tie a piece of azinheira to the pedestal of the statue in memory of the event at Fatima in 1917 when our Lady's feet rested lightly on the tops of the leaves of that kind of tree. Irmã Dores knew where there were some azinheiras. I joined her and Mother Cunha-Mattos in a trek up the garden walk and through a lane into the woods of the farm. There we came upon two azinheiras. One was rather small, and I broke off what seemed to me a branch long enough. It was not satisfactory for Irmã Dores, though, and she pointed to a larger one on the other tree. I reached up and ripped this long branch from the trunk.

Mother Superior and Irmã Dores carried the branches back. I preceded them. When I turned to speak with them, I wished so much that I could have a motion picture of this scene, both sisters carrying branches of a tree, Irmã Dores's branch very large, and Mother Superior's very small. Both of them smiled and laughed like children on a picnic.

When we returned to the proper location, Irmã Dores measured the branch she had brought against the stand. Seeing that it was too long, she broke it over her knee at the desired length. She twisted the parts to and fro with ease, hardly moving her elbows, until the bark was broken. She then tied the azinheira to the pedestal for the remaining photographs.

Little Teresa Barros-Gomes lent me her small camera when my few remaining films were exhausted, and with this I took several more photographs of Irmã Dores and the statue, and then of a little child standing beside the azinheira. This was suggested by Irmã Dores, to show the height of the children at the time of the apparition.

Her part in the modeling of the statue now complete, Irmã Dores returned to the building and to her silent tasks.

The casting remained to be done. For this operation I had the assistance of a sculptor of Vila Nova de Gaia named Armando Andrade. Many of the sisters watched this final phase of the work, but the one most interested was unable to attend because of the presence of a stranger. When the delicate and sometimes dangerous operation began, Mother Cunha-Mattos informed me that Irmã Dores was in the chapel praying for its success.

"She will be there a long time, if she stays until this is done," I warned Mother Superior. "Maybe you had better tell her."

Later in the afternoon, Mother Superior informed me that Irmã Dores was back at her work, sewing, but still praying. "Pray you also," she added. Mother King and I laughed. We had to explain that the expression was entirely grammatical but unusual in construction. This hardly seemed to clarify the reason for our mirth, but Mother Cunha-Mattos said she was happy to see us amused.

We worked in the yard until the darkness made it necessary to move the work up to the studio. It was late when the last piece in the mold was chipped away from the cast.

The hands and heart had to be formed separately and later attached. Most of the work was done by Senhor Andrade. No two sculptors cast exactly in the same manner, and since I could not convey, even through interpreters, the technical ideas necessary for dictating my preference, it became necessary to acquiesce in his. His work, I am happy to say, was flawless.

Only one part of the casting was entirely mine, and that was the little image of the heart surrounded by thorns.

In this "waste-mold process" of casting, the clay original is usually destroyed by being removed from the mold. However, the head and shoulders in this instance emerged unharmed. I prepared this head for firing in a kiln, by making a level base below the shoulders and hollowing it out. Then, with Mother Provincial's permission, I gave it to Irmã Dores.

In the morning I attached the hands and heart in what I thought were the proper places. After the plaster had set I wondered if possibly I might have placed the right arm in a position a little more to the center than it had been before it was detached in the clay. While I was going over the statue, retouching it, Irmã Dores came in to examine it. She seemed pleased but then concentrated on the right hand and said that it seemed a little too much toward center. She misses nothing! But, she added, "Don't change it now; it will be all right." Since all of the other details had been executed strictly according to her direction in every respect, I could not leave knowing that the position of an arm was in the least at variance with her description. I took a steel tool, cut into the plaster and broke the arm off; then I mixed fresh plaster in preparation for a new joining and asked Irmã Dores to hold it herself in the position that she wanted. This she did. The operation required her holding it steadily until the plaster set, a period of about two or three minutes.

The work had been trying, but the reward was very great—the joy of seeing Irmã Dores pleased. Toward the end of the modeling she had said, "Although it has been a lot of work, it is worthwhile to get it right." It was indeed worthwhile, not only to have arrived at a fairly accurate representation of the vision of Our Lady of Fatima but also to have achieved in the process a rather pleasing sculptural design. The composition was not mine at all. It was in every respect that of Irmã Dores. The execution alone, and that under all of the specifications and corrections given me by Irmã Dores, could be considered proper to my own efforts.

I shall always think of this as "our statue." The success that it has had cannot be explained by artistic skill of mine, but rather must be accounted for by the spiritual skill of the little child who saw Our Lady at Fatima.

12

SAUDADES

Saudades is, no doubt, the most expressive word in Portuguese and untranslatable. At least, this is the impression I gather from the explanation given by Mother Provincial before my departure from Sardão. The dictionary says it means "yearning, longing, regards, and greetings." Apparently it means all of these things and much more. It means: I had a wonderful time; I am very fond of you; I retain the most delightful memories from my visit; I wish you every conceivable blessing; I hope it will not be long before we meet again; you have been very kind to me; may happy days ever be with you, your friends, and your relations; "parting is such sweet sorrow"— just about every sentiment that friends can feel or express at the moment of farewell. When you put *muitas* in front of *saudades*, all of these feelings are intensified. The meaning of *muitas, muitas saudades!* therefore, simply defies analysis.

Muitas, muitas saudades! were exchanged at my departure. My stay had not only had the qualities of a most agreeable surprise and the fascination of working with Irmã Dores on an extraordinary project, but it had brought about some of the pleasantest associations I have known, in the sisters of the Colégio, both the mothers and the lay sisters, in the pupils, and in my newly acquired friends of Oporto.

Only the severe cold and dampness of an exceptional winter weighed against impressions of a perfect sojourn. Except for a few hours on a few days, the sun was not visible in all my stay. Rains that season were phenomenal and flooded many parts of Portugal. There was no heating equipment in the airy priest's house. But even this frigidity, which I sensed throughout my visit, occasioned some of the touches of human care and kindness that entered into the meaning of *saudades*.

Children and sisters alike were concerned about my coughing during Mass. Little Teresa Barros-Gomes sent cough drops to me. Irmã Dores gave me medicine on a spoon, before I could have my tea. The sisters sent a salve for my hands, which had been badly chapped from working in the wet clay. The little elderly lay sister who took care of my apartment always provided a ceramic hot-water jug for my feet. Every morning there was a brazier of hot charcoal brought upstairs by this same sister with the help of Irmã Dores's niece, Irmã Maria Amelia. Sometimes Irmã Dores herself took the place of the older nun. Mother King and Irmã Assunção brought me a toddy every night made of brandy and hot milk. Whatever calefactory or curative powers these things had, I am sure that the greater therapy was in the attention with which they were administered.

The brazier presented a problem. Fumes from the charcoal were quite dangerous, I was told, and I should always leave a window open to make sure that I had sufficient oxygen. Opening the window, of course, admitted more of the fresh, cold, damp air and nullified the effect of the fire. I had daily to gauge my minimum oxygen requirements against my maximum fume capacity to get a modicum of warmth.

For recreation I could always look forward to pleasant times in the dining room in the company of Mother King, and each dish brought with it Irmã Assunção with her witty instructions and commentaries in Portuguese and her beautiful laughter. I am indebted to Mother King for these friendly hours at the Colégio during which I learned much that has been of value in my understanding of Fatima and in my appreciation of Irmã Dores, whom Mother King knows so well. In many ways she confirmed the impressions that I acquired, and that many others had reported, of Irmã Dores's keen intelligence, perfect simplicity and naturalness, habitual reserve, and quick, sensitive humor.

Until my last day at Sardão I saw the children of the school only in chapel or when passing by classrooms or the children's dining room on the same floor with mine. I liked to hear them at recreation, noisy and gay as a treeful of birds on a spring morning. On Saturday, the day before I left, I chanced to meet them during their recreation in the garden yard. Gathered about their headmistress, they plied me with all sorts of questions, sometimes using the Barros-Gomes girl for interpreter but usually practicing the English that they daily studied. At their request I brought the statue, completed just an hour before, down from the studio. There was a chorus of "*Muito bonito!*" and "*Gosto muito!*" ("Very pretty," and "I like it very much.") I thought it admirable that these children, who see Irmã Dores daily but have been asked not to discuss her, had no inquiries or comments to make about the principal sculptor.

Their initial general curiosity about the United States soon became specific in their inquiries about Hollywood and "swing" music. They were more interested, however, in my own reaction to Portugal and were delighted to know that I liked their country very much. They are passionately patriotic. Although others may consider Portugal a small nation, there is certainly no question that the Portuguese regard it as the greatest place on earth.

It occurred to me that I had a splendid opportunity for entertainment if I could persuade the children to sing. Persuasion, however, was quite superfluous. I hardly mentioned my wish when dozens of suggestions flew about my head for a decision on the first number. The hymns of Fatima came first, then Portuguese folk songs, and finally their national anthem, all sung beautifully, in harmony. They provided encores without even waiting for the demand, but my enjoyment of the performance was manifest. "Do you want to see some Portuguese folk dances?" they asked. Of course I did. Then, under a great magnolia tree, at the side of the garden walk, their chosen representatives demonstrated several dances somewhat like our Western square dances.

This entertainment, I found out, was not to be entirely gratis. I had to perform in return. It was almost incredible to them that I knew no "swing" numbers, but they accepted my attempts to render a few Negro Spirituals and Western songs. This happy hour mixed several important ingredients into the *saudades*.

Pleasant times with my English friends, the Symingtons, at their homes for tea and dinner and at luncheon with them and their associates, further brightened these days and broadened the understanding I was gaining of the extent and depth of devotion to Our Lady of Fatima in Portugal. In these excursions from Sardão I was treated to considerable sightseeing in the picturesque cities of Vila Nova de Gaia and Oporto. From Englishmen as well as from Portuguese I learned more of the charm that is Portugal.

Everyone helped me with information about Fatima, especially two gentlemen whom I met through the Symingtons, Senhor José de Souza Guedes and Senhor Fernando d'Almeida. Senhor Souza Guedes is director of the hospital at Fatima and attends the pilgrimages on the thirteenth of each month, going down from Oporto. He had been associated with the Sanctuary from its inception and was well informed on all the cures of Fatima. I asked him how many of the cures he would consider to be evidently miraculous beyond question. He thought there were about three or four each year. That would mean a number beyond one hundred genuine miracles that have taken place at Fatima since the miracle of the sun in October 1917.

Senhor d'Almeida was a witness of the miracle of Maria José da Silva, of which Father Gardiner and Mr. Symington had spoken. He gave me his most interesting account of Maria's cure. He was one of the stretcher-bearers who had brought her from the hospital in a dying condition to the place of the sick at the steps of the basilica and was beside her when she arose from a stretcher and declared her own cure. We shall see more of his testimony when we arrive at the discussion of this miracle.

Toward the end of my stay at Sardão, Mother Provincial presented to Father Gardiner and me rosaries made by Irmã Dores. When I had seen her making the rosary for the statue I had hoped that I might have one made by her for myself. I had expressed the wish to Mother Corte Real. Irmã Dores was present when the rosaries were presented, but apparently her presence was forgotten by Mother Cunha-Mattos, for she explained to Father Gardiner in Portuguese that the beads of the rosaries were seeds from a tree that Irmã Dores had planted in Spain. Evidently, Mother Superior had brought the seeds with her from Spain. Irmã Dores could not help hearing. The reference to the seeds drew out a protest from her: "What special value does that give them?"

Afterward, Irmã Dores handed me two lined pieces of paper on which there was writing. I looked and recognized the prayers revealed by our Lady and the angel that I had asked her to write out for me.

On the eve of my departure, Mother Provincial asked me to bless the statue in the chapel. This, I thought, should be done rather by the chaplain of the Colégio, but when the time came, he was not present and the duty devolved necessarily upon me.

All the sisters and students were present. I placed the statue on the altar cloth in front of the tabernacle of the Blessed Virgin's altar at the epistle side of the chapel and there read the form for the blessing of images. Benediction was to follow; I crossed to the Sacred Heart altar at the other side to expose the Blessed Sacrament. As I ascended the step to open the tabernacle there was a thrilling, triumphant burst of song acclaiming *Nossa Senhora de Fatima*. It was the first honor paid to the newly blessed image.

Mr. Symington was coming Sunday morning to drive Father Gardiner and me to Fatima. At breakfast Mother King conveyed a surprise request from Mother Provincial. I was asked to join with Irmã Dores in an act of consecration to the Immaculate Heart of Mary, before the new image. I agreed, but I was puzzled and asked what was expected of me. Then I was told to use any form I wished and simply make an act of consecration. There was no form available in English, so I wrote one. Mother King brought it to Mother Provincial, who then translated it into Portuguese for Irmã Dores. The convent bell rang to call the community to chapel. Irmã Dores was outside the chapel doors holding her copy of the act of consecration when I arrived with my statue. There was a little delay as the sisters gathered from different parts of the house and entered the chapel. During this time Irmã Dores was gazing at the statue.

I had formerly accepted as quite sufficient the expressions of satisfaction evident in her attitude toward the work and also in her statements made to others concerning the statue. But now I wanted some word of final approval from Irmã Dores directly. An important word I had learned was the verb *gostar*, which means "to like" or "to be pleased with." *Gosta?* suffices for asking, "Do you like it?" and *Gosto* means "I like it." Now, with unprecedented daring, I inquired of Irmã Dores: "*Gosta?*" She replied with a smile and the greatest compliment ever given to the statue: "*Gosto.*"

I knelt at the Blessed Virgin's altar. The statue was again before the tabernacle. Irmã Dores took her place in the community. Father Gardiner and Mr. Symington knelt on prie-dieus in front. In the name of all, I read the act of consecration to the Immaculate Heart.

There was a moving and exciting little scene in the dining room, where the sisters gathered for the final visit. The nuns presented me with little holy cards inscribed with good wishes and assurances of prayers. A large, beautiful picture of our Lady conveyed the fond farewell of the entire community. The lay sisters who had waited on me both in caring for the apartment at the priest's house and attending table came to wish me well and to ask forgiveness for any faults or failures of which they might have been guilty, none of which the most exacting tyrant ever could have discerned. It was then that Mother Provincial explained the meaning of *saudades*.

Irmã Dores was in the room, but she did not take part in the conversation. She was very busy at a task that she had asked to perform, packing "our statue" in the little box. She worked silently, padding the little plaster image very gently with tissue paper. Then she closed the box, put the strap around it, and stood holding it until we left. She did not yield the case until we got into the car outside the gate.

There were half a dozen sisters standing in the gateway as we drove off. Irmã Dores was in the center, smaller than the rest. She held her hand highest and longest in that backhand wave peculiar to Europeans.

There was for all, at this leave-taking, I felt, an unseen participant in these *saudades*, the Lady of the "sweet but sad" countenance, who is "all of light."

13

THE BISHOP'S DECISION

We had a beautiful day for this ride down nearly half the length of Portugal from Vila Nova de Gaia back to Leiria. Mr. Symington's car was an Anglia, the English offspring of the Ford, lighter and of lower horsepower than its parent. Although we took our time, the lightness of the car and the reading of the speedometer in kilometers rather than miles gave the impression of great speed. Sometimes, when I drove, we were going around "seventy," but in miles we were doing a reckless forty-five or so.

The scenery was more interesting than that which we had seen from the train on the way up ten days before. Sometimes, at high points, we could look out on great expanse of plains and see the floods caused by the extraordinary rains of the past two weeks. The way was dotted with small towns, built often on hills, that made the cobbled road rise and fall through many charming views of streets, lined with bright, red-roofed houses.

It was carnival time. In every town children were out in force for their traditional fun. Dressed in brilliant and weird costumes borrowed from their elders, they held paper streamers across the road to be broken by our car. The more daring would try to snatch previously broken streamers that were flying from the sides of the car.

The only city of size on the way was Coimbra. Its university, the first in the world, stood out poised serenely on the summit of the heights, overlooking the city and the surrounding fertile farmlands.

At a pleasant roadside spot we stopped to enjoy a picnic lunch that Mrs. Symington had prepared. People passed by on foot, donkey carts, bicycles, and a few in cars. To everyone, Father Gardiner and Mr. Symington would hold up the food they were eating and say something that I could not understand. It seemed an odd performance, and I asked enlightenment. With the conventional expression, "*É servido?*" ("Are you served?") they were offering a share of their lunch. In this land famed for the courtesy of its people, there are no strangers among wayfarers. Of course, I did wonder what would happen if someone stopped. The lunch would be shared, Mr. Symington said. But I gathered that it is also good manners to decline the offer.

The ride was a restful interlude after the work and excitement of Sardão and gave us time to reflect on recent events with a view to placing everything in perspective and to planning the activity ahead. We would soon see the bishop of Leiria again. We had to thank him for the privileges he had made possible and to ask his permission to use the photographs of Irmã Dores. We talked about an idea that came to me after the completion of the statue. I thought that the unusual origin of the statue and its consequent authenticity might incline the bishop to consider my making it for the basilica. That was a lot to hope for, but I had the encouragement of knowing that Irmã Dores was praying for it. I had asked her to the day before.

The spot I had in mind for the statue was the niche over the main doorway of the basilica, eighteen feet high, which would have to be filled with a statue to complete the facade of the building. I felt that if the idea could be presented to Catholics in the United States who are devoted to Our Lady of Fatima, the necessary funds could be raised so as to make it a perpetual symbol of American Catholic devotion to the Blessed Virgin at her newest great shrine. I was confident of American interest and generosity. The problem was to get the bishop interested enough in the statue to approve it for a gift.

We arrived at Leiria, and so did bad weather, late in the afternoon. The bishop was in a village twelve miles away for Confirmation. We set out to find him. Several miles out of Leiria we asked directions of a ragged goatherd and found the muddy lane that was the proper turnoff from the hard road. We had not gone far on this lane when we had to stop for an oncoming car. It was the bishop's. After the difficult maneuvers of letting the bishop's car pass and turning our own around, we followed the bishop back to Leiria.

In his reception room again, we told the story of the statue. When Father Gardiner stated that meeting Irmã Dores had been one of the most interesting experiences of his life, the bishop, in a sort of challenging tone, demanded, "Why?" Then he folded his arms and sat back complacently to hear Father Gardiner enumerate her admirable qualities. With each statement of Father Gardiner, the bishop would smile and nod his head approvingly.

Then Father Gardiner explained that I had taken pictures of Irmã Dores that I had agreed not to use without the bishop's approval. Permission was given.

That brought us to the statue. The bishop saw it. He said he liked it better than the one I had previously shown him; and that was all he said. He smiled and was gracious; but that proved nothing, because he is always smiling and gracious. I was so let down that I told Father Gardiner to omit mention of my grand idea; to thank the bishop, ask his blessing, and let us leave. But Father Gardiner insisted that it would do no harm to ask, so I let him.

The bishop's answer was that he would accept a copy of my statue for a niche inside the basilica, but that work had already started on the one for the large niche outside. That was quite enough, however, to make me very happy. There was now the possibility that I would make a marble copy of the statue for Fatima itself.

I inquired about the miraculous cures at Fatima and asked if one could see the files on them at the hospital. The bishop said that it was his policy to leave the investigation of alleged miracles to the bishops of the dioceses to which the persons cured belonged. Only two miracles had been investigated at Fatima, he said.

Other questions that we had intended to ask the bishop before our previous visit had already been answered by Irmã Dores. We thanked the bishop, therefore, knelt for his blessing, and then left for the Cova da Iria.

It was cold and raining when we reached the top of the Serra and Mr. Petracchi's inn at the Cova. The Petracchis listened with great interest as my companions told them what had taken place at Vila Nova de Gaia. I could not share much of the reporting because there was work to be done on the statue. The vibration of the car had loosened the plaster at the joining in the right arm, which had been made by Irmã Dores the day before. It was not a serious matter. Wires held the forearm securely and in the position determined by Irmã Dores. Only a few bits of the fresh plaster had fallen from the joint. It was a development I had rather expected because the plaster had not had time to dry out well. I had brought along extra plaster and tools against this contingency. It required no more than half an hour's work. And I enjoyed thinking that I had already done some sculpturing at Fatima.

The weather in the morning did not look very promising for the principal objective of this second visit, which was to complete a set of photographs of the shrine and the places related to it. We had to wait often for the sun to come out. But the stormy skies fortunately turned out to be excellent backgrounds for many of the pictures.

When we arrived at the Sanctuary for Mass, there was a rainbow in the west, over the hospital. Later, when we were on the hilltop beyond the village of Fatima, a long rainbow with a very flat trajectory seemed to cover half the horizon of the Serra d'Aire. From this point we could look down over an olive orchard on the little village of Fatima at the crossroads. It seemed to be made up of a small circle of white houses around the pointed spire of the parish church. On the crest of the rock-covered hill to the northwest, sail-like blades of windmills were churning in front of the clouds over ancient, circular, stone structures. Off to the west, nearly two miles away, a beam of sunlight caught and illuminated the basilica against a slate-gray sky.

We visited the cemetery near the church in Fatima where Jacinta and Francis are buried and photographed their common grave. It stands near the gateway of the red clay acre. It is of weather-stained sandstone and like a sarcophagus, with a canopy at the head. Beneath this canopy there were various holy pictures and devotional objects. It was here in 1935, fifteen years after her burial at Vila Nova d'Ourem, that the body of Jacinta was found to be incorrupt.

In the afternoon, besides wanting to take more photographs of the shrine, I had a sentimental mission to perform. I carried my statue and a bundle of rosaries that I had obtained from Irmã Dores's sister Maria to the Chapel of the Apparitions to place them on top of the column that marks the spot where the apparitions occurred in 1917. It seems that the chapel is never entirely deserted. Now there was a little girl kneeling in a puddle of water on the rough concrete of the porch, poorly protected in a thin dress and veil from the sharp wind that crossed the Cova. Her eyes were radiant as she looked fixedly toward the niche inside the little chapel, while the beads moved slowly through her fingers.

A boy interrupted our picture-taking with the news that the bishop had come from Leiria and wanted to see the priest from the United States. He led the way to the retreat house, where the bishop was waiting in the office of Father Amilcar, chaplain of the shrine. The chaplain and another priest were with the bishop when we entered the room.

The bishop spoke. Father Gardiner interpreted. I was incredulous. I asked Father Gardiner to repeat. The bishop had said that he was considering asking me to make the statue for the great niche in the tower over the doorway of the basilica!

I took the statement literally and assumed that persuasion was in order to move him from consideration to decision. The immediate and obvious difficulty about the statue that I had made under the direction of Irmã Dores was that it differed from the familiar image at the Chapel of the Apparitions. I argued that in the statue that is to be the focal point of the Sanctuary it was fitting to have the representation of the Immaculate Heart, the

June apparition. The conventional image, with the hands of our Lady joined in prayer, shows *how* our Lady appeared at Fatima. In the gesture of the June apparition there is, in effect, a declaration of *why* she appeared, to call the world to penance, reparation, and salvation through devotion to her Immaculate Heart.

The bishop and the priests with him nodded agreement with the thought. Then I discovered that his "consideration" had been only a manner of speech, that he had come to tell me definitely that he wanted me to carve the statue for the tower.

I was deeply moved at this development, and Father Gardiner, who was quite as surprised and pleased as I was, conveyed my thanks to the bishop with appropriate emotional overtones.

We all then went for a walk to the basilica. In the courtyard between the retreat house and the hospital the bishop posed agreeably for photographs. I will always remember the day of the bishop's decision as a day of rainbows. Immediately on leaving the courtyard and entering the open space of the Cova proper, we saw the third rainbow of the day, a glorious band of almost flaming color against a black cloud.

During the walk I sought to get from the bishop some sidelights on the miraculous phenomena of Fatima. I asked if he had ever seen any. Very casually he remarked that he saw the shower of flowers when he first came to the Cova. I inquired when that was. He could not remember, exactly, he said. I thought then of the fountain, the water of which is commonly called miraculous. In a very arid region where nearly everyone subsists on rainwater gathered in cisterns, it is popularly considered a miracle that springs were discovered in the center of the Cova when workmen had dug only a few feet in preparation for building a cistern. The water from the springs is now stored in the central fountain and used by pilgrims. Several cures have been attributed to its use.

"What about the water, Bishop; is it miraculous?" He answered abruptly, "*Agua natural!*" (natural water).

However much we may wish for further exposition of the wonders that have occurred at Fatima, it may be that in the long run the extreme caution of the bishop in this respect, which amounts almost to detachment, will be an asset to the credibility of Fatima for the world at large. No one will ever be able to accuse the bishop of Leiria of having exaggerated the miraculous at Fatima. He is ardently devoted to Fatima itself, but the miracles that are of greatest importance to him are the moral wonders that melt hardened hearts and bring thousands to their knees in this place of penance.

Standing with us in the nave of the great church, he told us that the huge barrel vault was completely of stone construction. It covered a space that, he said, could accommodate eight thousand worshippers. The workmen who were laying the floor were the first outside craftsmen employed; the rest of the work had been done by local labor. The stone was from local quarries.

"When will it be finished?" I inquired.

With unconcerned patience he replied that he did not know. He explained that the building is being paid for with completely unsolicited donations that come from all over the world. As funds are available, the work goes ahead; there is no construction timetable.

Father Gardiner and I left the bishop to visit the foundry, a long shedlike building, inside which, in deep pits, the bells were being forged to complete the carillon of the tower. The forms or profiles of the bells, known as templates, were being shaped by craftsmen out of wood. With these the workmen would make the clay molds into which the bronze would be poured. Smoke from the pit fires nearly choked and blinded us, and we wondered how these men could survive it all day long. Since I had just become a potential worker at the Cova myself, I felt a special fraternity with these craftsmen. They were very friendly and tried to explain bell forging to me. But their explanations were too rapid for full interpretation. It did not matter, I felt; when I came back, I would speak their language and come to know them by name.

We met the bishop again at the Chapel of the Apparitions, to which I returned to fulfill the intention that had brought me there earlier. He blessed the statue and my rosaries at the very spot where our Lady had appeared. He said a prayer in the chapel and then gave us his blessing and returned to Leiria.

That evening I cabled to New York the news about the statue. There were four persons whom I wanted to inform as quickly as possible: my parents; my superior, Father T. S. McDermott, O.P., Provincial; and Mr. John E. Rigali, President of the Daprato Statuary Company of Chicago. Father McDermott had not only arranged this trip for me, but from my ordination to the priesthood in 1932 he had made possible my education, occupation, and continuation in the unusual capacity of sculptor-priest. The contract that my good friend Mr. Rigali had offered me the previous summer had occasioned my trip to Fatima.

Two important objectives remained for the next day. I wished to photograph the entire Cova from the top of the bell tower and to visit and photograph Valinhos, the place where our Lady appeared on August 19, 1917, and the spot known as the Cabeço, the grotto where the angel appeared to the children in 1916.

The first of these deeds would better have been done by a professional steeplejack. The tower is 220 feet to the crown and is reached, in the last stages, by almost vertical ladders. The climb was made no simpler by the habit I wore and the cameras and light meter I carried. My guide, the Italian lay brother who was the sacristan at the Chapel of the Apparitions, called back to me from the crown as I stood near the low sill of an open archway at the foot of the last ladder and warned me to be careful of a loose rung. Safe at the top, I had to contend with a numbing wind that came through the ribs of the crown as I took views of the Cova and its surrounding structures.

Mr. Symington drove us to Aljustrel before he went on his way back to Oporto. There was mutual regret at his having to leave for we had shared many pleasant and interesting experiences. He brought with him our *saudades* to the sisters at Sardão and our other friends in Oporto as well as the news of the bishop's decision.

We then called on a niece of Irmã Dores in Aljustrel and asked her to direct us to Valinhos and the Cabeço. She sent her little daughter, four years old, to be our guide and assured us that she was well informed and knew the way perfectly. The child was exceptionally bright, very sweet, and completely unafraid of strangers. She chatted merrily as we walked along a rocky lane, each of us holding a hand; and she laughed happily whenever we lifted her over the weeds in the middle of the road.

I had always thought of Valinhos as an inhabited place. It was only a spot in a lonely field, half a mile west of the village of Aljustrel. A small pile of stones like a well marked the spot where our Lady had appeared. People had devoutly left a little statue in the well and surrounded it with branches of azinheira. Farther on, up a hill, we came to the rocky formation known as the Cabeço. It is not a cave but a deep hollow in the rocks. Our little guide pointed to the tall rock on which the angel had stood.

On our return to Aljustrel we had only a very little time before our departure for Lisbon. We met the parents of Jacinta and Francis, Ti and Tia Marto, and took pictures of them with two of their little grandchildren who were named after Francis and Jacinta. In the few minutes we could be with them, we listened not to their description of the little ones whom our Lady had taken to heaven, but to their proud account of the many religious vocations in the Marto family.

When we left the Cova to go down into the valley for the train, this time back to Lisbon, much more than we had planned had come to pass. The basilica remained in view for a long time, and I kept looking at the tower and thinking of the great niche over the doorway, which would, I hoped, bring me back again.

14

THE CURE OF MARIA DA SILVA

Many people miss God's point about miracles. He does not ask us to believe in miracles; He hits us between the eyes with them. He demands that we believe in *Him* and in everything He has made known. To convince us that He is making something known, He does what only the Creator of nature can do—He makes visible creation act in a manner that differs from its naturally fixed behavior. He confronts us with eye-opening facts. He says, in effect: "Look here, and pay attention; I have something to tell you. Listen to me!"

Now, in the absence of evidence, we don't have to worry about what an alleged happening may mean. We can believe what God says only when we are sure that He has spoken. We are sure that He has spoken when we have conclusive evidence of a miracle in support of a claim that He has spoken. We have to examine carefully the proofs of reported miracles. If the proofs are satisfactory, that's that. God has acted. We go on from there to inquire about the significance of His action. If the proofs are inadequate, we forget the whole matter.

For instance, nobody asks us to combine the miracles and the message of Fatima into one great dose of believing that is too big to swallow. We are asked to accept the message because of the miracles. If we are not convinced of any miracle at Fatima, we are quite free to suspend judgment about the message. The seventy thousand people who saw the sun perform so strangely on October 13, 1917, did not say, "My word! I believe this is a miracle." They knew very well it was. What they said was: "My God! I believe in You!" When little Lucy dos Santos was lifted up by a man named Carlos Mendes and asked to tell the people what our Lady had said, she did not have to explain that if they believed God had worked a miracle they could believe our Lady had said thus and so. After God's preface to the child's statement, they were simply interested in knowing the contents of the "thus and so."

We have already learned the contents of the message of Fatima from Lucy herself. We have had also some evidences of the miracles with which God confirms that message. In the week that remained of my stay in Portugal I inquired further about such evidences.

One miracle takes as much omnipotence as a thousand. If one becomes a fact for us, then we have to accept the message that it sustains. Of course, many miracles make the message more emphatic. That is just what God has done at Fatima. He has given the message of the Blessed Virgin tremendous emphasis. Senhor Souza Guedes made the very conservative estimate of about a hundred certainly miraculous cures at the Cova. There was at least one miracle during each pilgrimage at Fatima from

May to October in 1946; and there were three on one day, May 13, 1946. The volume of Fatima wonders is very well known in Portugal, but, unfortunately, very little known in the United States. A few miracles have been described in some of the books on Fatima published in English, and every history of Fatima duly accents the miracle of the sun of October 13, 1917; but we need very much a work that will give a more extensive and critical presentation of Fatima miracles. I do not propose to fill that need in these chapters but only to report on particular evidences that I personally encountered.

During my stay in Portugal I met two persons who were miraculously cured at Fatima. I will present the stories of their cures. Nearly everyone I met told me about the miracle of the doves of December 1946. It is a simple, charming story about a very real and very recent prodigy. I have already given the testimony of Teresa and Maria, Irmã Dores's sisters, on the miracle of the sun; this testimony will be augmented by accounts I received from two other persons, one of them Senhor Carlos Mendes. Although these testimonies are sufficient proof, I cite them with the reminder that my witnesses are only four out of seventy thousand who saw the miracle of the sun. These are the evidences I offer, not in any sense as the total argument for the credibility of Fatima, but as segments for which I can vouch of the great body of proof that exists in Portugal.

Maria José da Silva was instantly cured of a grave abdominal infection on May 13, 1946. Father Gardiner and both Mr. John and Mr. Ronald Symington saw the miracle take place. The Symingtons had me meet Senhor Fernando d'Almeida in Oporto because he assisted Maria as her stretcher-bearer, was at her side when the cure occurred, and kept in touch with her after the cure.

When I told Senhor d'Almeida that I would like to meet Maria and learn more of her case, he wrote to Senhora Patricio, the nurse who was with Maria at the time of her cure, to advise her that I would call and to ask her both to explain the case to me and to accompany me to Carrazedes so that I might meet Maria.

John Stilwell came with me to the home of Senhora Patricio in Lisbon on February 23, 1947, and interpreted for me. The following is a summary of the information I received from Senhora Patricio.

Senhora Patricio first met Maria at the Hospital of the Cova da Iria on the morning of the thirteenth of May 1946.

Maria had undergone an appendectomy on April 22, 1942, in the Hospital of São José in Lisbon. Eighteen days after the operation the wound had suppurated. Treatment by many doctors in several hospitals had failed to improve her condition. She had two great sores, one in her abdominal wall, the other in her left arm, occasioned by an injection. Senhora Patricio described Maria's state as pitiable. In the infirmary of the hospital, her wounds had been scraped and cleaned and new dressings placed on them. Despite her weakness she pleaded to see the procession of our Lady's statue. With Senhora Patricio's help, she painfully walked, stumbling, to the window.

"The smell was simply too frightful for words," Senhora Patricio stated.

By a happy coincidence, the statue stopped in the procession for a moment in front of the window where they were standing.

"Ask our Lady to cure you," Senhora Patricio said.

Maria replied, "Faith does not fail me," then leaned her head on her nurse's shoulder. When the procession passed on, Senhora Patricio had to have the assistance of another nurse to put her patient to bed. She was extremely weak, so weak that when a doctor passing by asked, "How are you getting on?" she could not reply at all. The doctor then remarked to Senhora Patricio that if our Lady cured Maria, it would be one of the greatest miracles of Fatima.

The exertion of going to the window had a telling effect on her condition. Senhora Patricio was alarmed and called the doctor. He ordered an injection of camphorated oil to revive Maria's heart action.

Most of the patients had gone out before Maria. The trip of a few hundred yards to the place of the sick at the base of the basilica steps further weakened her heart. I asked Senhora Patricio if Maria had gone into a coma. She replied, "Somewhat, with lucid moments." She told me that a doctor complained to her, "Why have you brought this girl out? She's not at all fit to be here." Senhora Patricio answered, "That is why she came to Fatima."

On arrival her stretcher was placed in the last position. Her nurse gave her water and then called the doctor again. He gave a second injection.

The official in charge of the sick decided to move the stretcher cases ahead of the patients who were sitting. In the shuffle Maria's position turned out to be in the first row, directly in the center of the stairway.

Her condition grew worse during the Mass, and she had to be wrapped in a blanket. Senhora Patricio described Maria's state: "She was feverish and gasping; she was overcome by lassitude and pulled distractedly at her clothing; her eyes rolled upward." Senhora Patricio gave her water periodically; another nurse administered smelling salts. After a while Senhora Patricio stopped giving Maria water because she was not swallowing anymore.

At one point Senhora Patricio thought that Maria was dead. Her respiration was too weak for observation, but then the nurse noticed a pulsation in an artery of her neck. Maria's face began to swell. Another doctor was called. He ordered an injection. Then the first doctor came and canceled the order, declaring that he had just given her one.

In a lucid moment Maria gasped, "I can't stand it anymore; the blessing is taking so long." When the cardinal legate arrived with the monstrance containing the Blessed Sacrament, for the individual blessing of the sick, Senhora Patricio lifted Maria's head and told her, "The Blessed Sacrament is in front of you now." Senhora Patricio told me that she believed at the time Maria could hear, although she could not speak. Maria remembers nothing of these things.

These are Senhora Patricio's words describing the miracle:

> As the Blessed Sacrament came in front of Maria she suddenly leaped up, unassisted, and said "I am cured! Nothing hurts me!" The crowd immediately became excited and surrounded her. She was forced to sit down again. The cardinal of Lisbon, seeing what had happened, ordered everyone to move away, then gave her a special blessing himself. Maria wanted to walk back to the hospital, but the excitement of the crowd was so great that the nurse had to pretend that she was taking her back because of her illness. The arm that had suffered before so that it was useless she now had around the neck of her stretcher-bearer.

> She could hardly be restrained in her joy. The doctors warned her, "Keep quiet, this may not be a miracle." In the hospital the bandages were removed. The infections had disappeared.

Senhora Patricio added that after the cure had been recognized by the doctors, Maria walked about for two hours as though nothing had ever been wrong. She went to the Chapel of the Apparitions to pray and wandered through the crowd in search of her family. On the following day, the doctor in her village removed the bandages and, finding them perfectly clean, replaced them. Two days later Dr. Mendes examined her at Torres Novas and found the wounds closed and healing.

After this interview I asked Senhora Patricio to write a statement in my notebook to the effect that she had given me this eyewitness testimony. She wrote the following declaration:

> As a Servita of the girl who was miraculously acted upon on the 13th of May, 1946, I hereby certify that I was a witness to everything which transpired before and after the miracle, and I further certify to the truth of everything I told Rev. Fr. McGlynn on this 23rd day of February of 1947.
>
> *(Signed)* Maria da Guia Felicio Patricio

I had asked Mr. John Symington (brother of Mr. Ronald Symington) in Oporto if he would write out his account of the cure. He had told me that he had written one soon after witnessing the miracle and offered to make a copy of it for me. It follows:

> There have been many cases of remarkable miracles at Fatima for many years, but I would like to describe my own experience of a wonderful miracle that I had the

privilege of witnessing last Monday, the thirteenth of May, at Fatima. I had been helping to carry the sick from the hospital to their place in the open below the steps of the church, and when the sick were all in position I placed myself behind one of the patients. She was a young girl of twenty-one, and it was quite obvious from her appearance that she was desperately ill. She looked as if she might die at any moment. A friend of mine, Mr. Fernando Almeida, who had carried her down on a stretcher, was standing beside her mattress and next to me, so I asked him what she was suffering from, and he told me that her case was a desperate one of T.B. and that she had had altogether six operations, and he feared that she might not last out the Mass. The girl was in a state of coma and quite unconscious of what was going on around her, and her face was a ghastly color and wore a look of suffering though apparently unconscious.

For three quarters of an hour I stood behind her mattress and I kept on looking at her, for I was concerned about her. Then a doctor ordered an injection to be given her, and a nurse kept taking her pulse, but when a nurse arrived with a syringe to give her an injection, a doctor decided it should not be given, as apparently she had just had an injection shortly before. At the end of High Mass the cardinal legate came down the steps from the altar carrying the Blessed Sacrament and commenced blessing the sick. This girl was the second patient to be blessed. He blessed her with the Blessed Sacrament while she lay unconscious, and he was just moving to the next mattress on the ground when, as I raised my head as the Blessed Sacrament passed on, I saw this girl slowly but firmly rise to a sitting position, and she started to speak and to say that she wanted to get up, for she was all right.

I saw the cardinal stop and look back at her, and he then moved quietly on. Several people who were standing around then came up to have a look at her, and my brother, who was close by, also came up in time to see her getting up, and he heard her say that she was no longer in pain. She was persuaded not to get to her feet; otherwise the crowd in their excitement and enthusiasm might have crushed her. The cardinal patriarch, who was at the foot of the stairs and had noticed this remarkable miracle, then blessed her and smiled at her.

My friend Mr. Fernando Almeida and another person then carried her back to the hospital, where she was immediately reexamined by the doctors who had already seen her previously and who had registered her case (for none of the sick came down for the blessing before being duly examined and registered). About three-quarters of an hour later I saw, to my utter amazement, the same girl walking about and talking cheerfully and brightly to my friend Almeida. Her color had returned and she seemed in *perfect* health. I asked her several questions, and she said she felt absolutely all right. She told me she had been ill for five years and that for two years she had not been able to walk properly. All pain had completely gone and her left arm, which had been paralyzed, was now perfectly normal. The girl promised Almeida that she would write to him to let him know how things were going with her, and Almeida has promised to give me news of her. I asked another friend of mine, Mr. José Maria Souza Guedes, who was working in the hospital, what the doctors said, but

> he said the doctors would not pronounce anything at the moment. My friend told me unofficially that from their first impressions the case could not be more astounding or interesting.

On his typewritten manuscript Mr. Symington added the following in his handwriting:

> There were about 700,000 people at Fatima on the thirteenth of May 1946; that is approximately one-tenth of the population of Portugal.
>
> I declare that the account of this miracle is the absolute truth as I witnessed it myself and was written while details were still fresh in my memory, and I fully realize my great privilege.

Senhor d'Almeida's oral description of Maria's cure had been given to me one day at lunch in Oporto. At my request he put it in writing. This is not a translation; Senhor d'Almeida wrote in English:

> At about 12 p.m. on the thirteenth of May 1946, when all the patients at the Fatima Hospital were being taken to the place reserved for them at the bottom of the steps of the Basilica to attend Mass and Benediction, I was called, as stretcher bearer, to take down one of the very sick.
>
> As I entered the ward where she was and looked at the girl, I was greatly impressed by her appearance. I can only say that, to anybody, she looked more dead than alive.
>
> She seemed to be in "coma." Her eyes were closed, the greyishness of her colour was frightening, and one could hardly see her breathing. I remarked to the nurse that she looked very bad and was told that she had been

in that state during all the night—one of the worst cases that had come to Fatima to implore the blessing of God for their different ailments after having given up all hope of cure by modern science. She had been brought in, the night before, after a very painful journey.

As usual, she had been examined by the doctors at Fatima, and as she had two sores, one on the left arm and the other in the abdominal region, these were attended to and properly dressed. I was told that one in the abdomen was in communication with the intestines. The other was in such bad state that all the dead tissues had to be removed and scraped.

A very trying experience, as, they told me, the odor from the sores was something appalling.

I asked the nurse whether she could be safely transported to the Basilica and was told that all during the night she had taken some heart tonics and had just been given another injection. We started then on our way through that immense crowd, and I can only say that, on everybody who looked at her, we could clearly see an expression of pity.

It is difficult to describe the wonderful sight of Fatima that day when hundreds of thousands of people were gathered together, in a respectful and silent manner to assist at the Coronation of our Lady, by His Holiness the Pope's Legate.

It was difficult to make our way through that crowd, and we just managed to get along by calling the people's attention to the state of this girl. Even so, it took us about twenty minutes to cover a distance which is usually done in three. Many a time the stretcher had to be put down, and once this poor girl showed such signs of suffering that we half decided to take her back to the Hospital, lest she would die there and then.

Eventually, we got her amongst the other sick.

Her stretcher was placed in the front row so that she could be one of the first to receive Benediction, when Mass was finished. The only sign of life that could be detected was her constant gasping for breath. The nurse never left her side, and I kept very near in order to attend quickly to whatever was needed. She only asked for water and while drinking a few drops she showed such acute suffering that one of the Doctors was called.

All through Mass she did not show any signs of taking notice of what was going on.

Then came the solemn moment of the Benediction of the Blessed Sacrament for the sick. The Monstrance was held by the Cardinal Legate who, stopping in front of this girl, gave her the Blessing of Our Lord. Before anyone could realize what was happening, this girl opened her eyes and sat up on the stretcher.

The nurse tried to help her but she got up without any help, staring at the Blessed Sacrament and saying, "I am cured, I am cured!" She was asked, in vain, to lie down again and keep quiet, so as not to disturb the solemn ceremony. Even so, the word "miracle" was spread from mouth to mouth, and there was a certain commotion around.

As soon as possible she was taken back to the Hospital and it took some persuasion to prevent her from walking back all by herself. She had to be rushed through the crowd, which, having learned of this cure, was eager to see the lucky one.

Once back at the Hospital she jumped up and walked around the consulting room. She, who had not been able to walk for over five years or use her left arm, was now, in a paroxysm of joy, waving her arms about and showing how she had recuperated her movements!

She was at once examined by the Doctors, and I understood that, although the sores were not completely healed, they were so modified that they could be healed in a couple of days.

And so they were!

As a matter of fact, they were found to be healed the very next morning, when the dressings were removed by the local physician, at the small village where she lives, as she told me in a letter written two or three days later. To use her own expression, "only the scars remained as witnesses of my previous ailments."

After finding herself cured in the Hospital, her first thoughts were for her mother, who, lost in the crowd, had not yet known that her child was cured. She was called by means of the loud speakers, but this girl was so naturally impatient to see her mother, that she insisted on going out and looking for her. She told us, "I am well and can walk, so let me go and look for Mother." She could not only walk about like any of us, but she looked well. The colour of her face was quite natural, and [her face] was radiant with joy. It was then that I met my friends John and Ronald Symington, who can also witness this fact, and to whom she explained what had happened to her. I was told that the sore on her abdomen was in consequence of an operation for appendicitis, 5 years ago, and had never healed up since.

I have seen this girl frequently, looking the picture of health and feeling perfectly fit. One month later we met again at Fatima. This time, she was no more a sick girl imploring the protection of our Lady but working in the Hospital as one of the "Servitas." She told me that her miraculous cure had been the cause of many conversions in her village.

All this I solemnly declare to be the truth and seen by me on that memorable day of the thirteenth of May of the year of 1946.

(Signed) Fernando d'Almeida 28th Feb. 1947

On the last page of this document, at my request, the Symington brothers, both of whom had witnessed the miracle, made the simple declaration:

We witness the truth of this statement.

(Signed) John D. Symington
Ronald A. Symington

The doctor who attended Maria at Fatima before her cure and examined her immediately after the miracle was Augusto Mendes of the city of Torres Novas, a brother, incidentally, of Senhor Carlos Mendes, noted in the story of the events at Fatima in 1917. Torres Novas was on the way to Carrazedes, where Maria lives, in the vicinity of Fatima, to the east of the Serra d'Aire. On February 25 John Stilwell drove me, together with Senhora Patricio and a priest-reporter from the newspaper *Novidades*, to visit both Dr. Mendes and Maria.

Two incidents unrelated to miracles supplied unexpected excitement on the long trip. John Stilwell had been telling me about the famous bulls of Vila Franca de Xira. Bred through centuries for their ferocity for the bullfights of Vila Franca, they were quite the most savage animals alive, he said, and would attack anything that moved. As we neared the city, John stopped the car. Ahead of us and moving down the road toward us was a huge herd of the celebrated beasts he had been describing. They were very dark brown, had menacing horns, and all looked very angry as they were prodded on by horsemen with spears. A man ahead of us abandoned his bicycle and climbed a six-foot wall. When he saw me adjusting the lens of my camera, John gave me the superfluous advice that I had better stay in the car. All passed by, however, without incident beyond a few threatening glares.

Farther on, in lowlands that had been flooded, we came upon an interurban bus that had gone off the road, down a steep embankment, and was lying on its side, half submerged. Men seemed to be working excitedly, standing on the side of the bus. Survivors stood anxiously on the bank. For a moment I wondered how I would get around the language difficulty in the priestly ministrations I felt sure I would have to perform. Then I remembered that I was sitting beside a Portuguese priest. Happily no one was seriously hurt. Had the bus gone over the bank two feet sooner, it would have struck a culvert and capsized and would probably have drowned all the passengers.

After lunch in Torres Novas we went to the home of Dr. Mendes. He gave me the following account of the cure of Maria da Silva.

Dr. Mendes was on duty at the hospital at the Cova da Iria when Maria arrived there. He removed the dressings from her abdominal wound and from the wound on her left arm. There was so much suppuration on the bandages that it had gone through to her clothing. He asked how long she had had these bandages on. She replied that they had been placed on her the previous evening.

There were, he explained, three fistulae in her abdomen about seven centimeters deep that drained into an open wound four centimeters or nearly two inches long in the abdominal wall. There was a copious flow of pus. He remarked the same disgusting odor observed by Senhora Patricio. After cleaning the wounds, he applied fresh bandages before Maria was carried out to the Sanctuary.

On her return immediately after the cure, he noted the following changes. There was the complete disappearance of the pus. The wounds were dried up. There was no dead skin, although the wounds were still open. The bandages were perfectly clean and dry. The only residue of the former infection was a solid lump of what appeared to be white pus left on the bandage that covered her abdomen. There was no longer any odor.

I asked him if he would have expected the bandages to be moist. He replied that, judging from the moisture of the bandages from the previous day, there should have been a certain amount of pus.

At my request, he wrote out the following brief statement:

> The cure of the patient Maria José da Silva in May of 1946 cannot be explained clinically, but only by the rapid cessation of abundant suppuration and by the healing in a few days of the external wounds. I treated her on the thirteenth of May at the hospital of Fatima and observed her on the same day and three times in the Hospital of Torres Novas and in my own office.
>
> *(Signed)* Dr. Augusto Mendes,
Torres Novas 25th Feb. 1947

We found Maria in a hamlet beyond her own, where she had gone for a funeral. She was very happy to see Senhora Patricio and showed excited delight in having visitors from so far. She was round-faced and healthy looking and only horn-rimmed glasses kept her from appearing much younger than her twenty-one years.

We drove her back to Carrazedes, and I questioned her on the way. She told me that the journey to Fatima before her cure had been very painful. The village doctor had offered to take her in his car, but she had declined, preferring to ride in a donkey cart so that she could suffer more. I asked if she had always been a devout Catholic. She said that she had. She had received the last sacraments many times during her long illness. For a month before her cure she had received Holy Communion daily. She said that in going to Fatima she had asked for a cure but had made the alternate petition that, if she was not worthy of a cure, she be allowed to suffer more for her sins and then be taken.

After our return to Carrazedes, Maria showed us the small parish church and the shrine of Our Lady of Fatima, which, she proudly told us, it was her privilege to care for. She regretted very much that there could be no flowers, because it was Lent.

Her village had once been very irreligious, but conversions had been numerous since her cure and the people were now putting up a large building to be used for Catholic Action.

Maria wore a very large silver medal of Our Lady of Fatima that she said Senhor d'Almeida had given her.

It was not necessary now, after four accounts of her cure, to learn details from her. She did supply the information, however, that she had been ill for five years before her cure and had undergone six operations. She removed a faded purple corduroy jacket to show the large scar on her left arm where, before the miracle, there had been a fetid wound.

In the little time that we could visit, I took several pictures of Maria and had her sign my notebook.

We left Carrazedes and the joyful little *miraculada* toward sunset and drove away along the rocky road that Maria once traveled in pain on her way to Fatima. The long, even contour of Fatima's mountain range loomed dark against the reddening sky beyond the valley.

15

THE CURE OF NATALIA DOS SANTOS

Because my time in Portugal was limited, I had planned to inquire only about the miracle of Maria da Silva. But one evening at tea, when we were discussing the case of Maria, Mrs. Stilwell said that she had met in Lisbon a girl who had been cured at Fatima of an ear infection. She said that the girl had shown her the scar behind her ear where tissue had grown together over a mastoid wound. Mrs. Stilwell asked me if I would be interested in meeting this girl. I was, of course. Mrs. Stilwell said she would arrange it. A few days later I received a note from her giving me the address of Natalia dos Santos and explaining that although Natalia had been recently ill with a cold, she would be glad to see me.

A young man from Madeira whom I met at the hotel, Senhor Martim da Camara, had become interested in my work through seeing the statue and had offered to assist me if he could. I invited him to be my interpreter during the visit with Natalia.

After a shopping trip that took us to many stores in several of Lisbon's busy streets, we succeeded in finding metric rules that I would need for my work in planning the new statue for the basilica; then, at the central square, the Praça Rocio, we took a taxi to go to Natalia's home. The ride brought us into the older part of the city, the Moorish section, where the buildings seemed battered and piled together in ancient but picturesque disarray on very crooked, narrow, hilly streets. The taxi stopped at an apartment building. Through a worn doorway we entered a dark hall and went up three flights. Natalia answered the door.

She was a very pretty girl with a charming manner, tall and somewhat thin. Her dark, straight hair, combed back over her ears, accented the paleness of her complexion. She was serious but friendly. The neatness and severity of her attire were matched by the simplicity of her apartment.

We sat around a small table that was covered with a crocheted cloth, in the combination dining and living room. Natalia's speech was rapid; her expression was lively and pleasant but restrained.

I had Senhor Camara explain my purpose. I had come to inquire about her cure, not to be convinced myself—for I had accepted the fact on good authority—but to have evidence for people in the United States who are not acquainted with Fatima miracles.

Natalia began immediately to tell of another miracle. She went into the next room and returned with a book, explaining that she thought this would be just what I wanted, a study of a remarkable cure that she herself had seen occur. As a servita she had assisted the girl who was cured.

I said I knew well that there had been many miracles at Fatima but that I was especially interested in learning about hers. It would be more useful to be able to say on my return that I had met a person who had been cured than to say I had read an interesting account of a cure. It was only with a bit of insistence and with an assurance that I would accept a copy of the book that we got her away from the topic of the other cure and on that of her own.

I was soon to learn that, whereas Natalia had been reported as a wonderful case because she had been cured of mastoid infection, she had also been cured at the same time of blindness, partial deafness, and paralysis. Her case history was a story of most extraordinary suffering throughout all the twenty years of her life that preceded the miracle.

Natalia was born on January 3, 1917. She experienced health for the first time in her life at Fatima on May 13, 1937.

She was operated on at the age of three days for an infection of the middle ear. This was the first of sixteen operations by which doctors of Lisbon's São José Hospital strove futilely to overcome a mastoid infection.

Natalia described the illness as a continuous infection that involved her left ear, the mastoid bone behind her left ear, the left side of her skull, and the cheek and forehead sinuses of the left side of her face. I noticed straight, vertical scars at the sinuses above and below her left eye. She said there had been two open wounds, one high on the left side of her head and the other in back of her ear, left by a mastoidectomy. She had lost the sight of her left eye and the hearing of her left ear. The wounds of her head had never healed.

Natalia was in and out of São José Hospital continually before the cure, and, when at home, was always an invalid. She was continuously in the hospital from 1934 to 1936. Pus had issued from her ear all her life and, in the last years of her illness, also from her nose, the mastoid wound, and the wound on the side of her head.

The last of her operations was performed in January 1936. Fluid was drained from her spine to determine if she had meningitis. Soon afterward the symptoms of meningitis developed, as seen in the arching of the back, neck rigidity, and the pulling back of her arms in spastic paralysis. The vision of her right eye also became impaired so that she could see only blurs of light.

Natalia illustrated the position in which she was fixed for a year and a half by thrusting her elbows and head back as far as they would go.

After the last operation, Dr. Luis Alberto Mendonça, her surgeon, visited her daily for a while and then had an assistant look after her. Various treatments were finally abandoned as futile.

Another operation was recommended by Dr. Mendonça in October 1936. Natalia refused to submit to it and demanded to be allowed to go home. Dr. Mendonça did not want to release her, but she insisted. "Go, if you like," he said. "This is a hospital, not a prison or an asylum." Contrary to medical advice, she had her father bring her home in an ambulance on October 11, 1936.

Neighbors who saw her being carried into the house said that she had been brought home to die. At the sight of the blood on her dressings some bystanders became hysterical.

Natalia was hardly ever without acute pain for twenty years.

But physical pain was not all that she had to endure. Both in the hospital and at home, she was subjected to mental torture of diabolical character. She was devoutly Catholic, and her piety was a reproach to the irreligious lives of some of the nurses. They plagued her with blasphemous jest. They would make a dummy of a broomstick, pillows, and sheets and say to her, "There is your

Lady of Fatima!" When the priest came to bring Holy Communion they would plan the performance of unpleasant chores to coincide with his visit, in bold insult to the Real Presence. They took her rosary away and her Jocist, Catholic Action, emblem. Sometimes when she asked for water they would say, "Tell the priest to get your water!"[3]

Natalia was an infant when her mother died. Her father remarried. Natalia's stepmother had been a widow and had a grown daughter. Both mother and daughter mistreated and neglected her. A neighbor had to provide her with food and bed linens at times. The stepsister made fun of her affliction, said she was tired of working for her, and demanded that she get up and go to work herself. Once, her stepmother even threatened her with a knife.

There were some, however, who took pity on her, devout ladies who visited her in the hospital and at home, and urged her on to perseverance in prayer and patience. They encouraged her great devotion to the Blessed Virgin by telling her that, since she had never known her earthly mother, she should regard our Lady as her mother.

It was one of these ladies who arranged her journey to Fatima, Senhora Dona Maria José Attaide Mascarenhas.

In all her illness Natalia had made only one petition related to her physical condition. Because of the negligence of the nurses she had asked our Lady to give her the use of her right arm so that she could help herself to water. Her petition had not been granted.

When the opportunity came for her to go to Fatima, she gladly seized it. Yet, strangely, she had no thought at all of being cured.

[3] "All this has improved now that the hospital has a chaplain," observed Miss Molly Stilwell on reading this part of the manuscript.

She simply wanted to visit her "Mother." She knew that she could not see our Lady until she died, but she felt she would be near her at Fatima because our Lady had been there.

Natalia was clothed in her burial shroud for the journey, because she had no other dress. She was taken by Dona Maria in a pilgrimage of Catholic Youth. Wrapped in blankets, she made the journey by train, lying on the floor of the car between the seats. The movement of the train caused her severe pain, which remained with her all through that night of May 12, 1937, while she was in the hospital at Fatima.

In the morning Natalia received Holy Communion. She was extremely weak. She was dazed, and at the Mass of the Sick she did not realize that she was at Fatima. During the prayers her servita, Senhora Dona Margarida Tarouca, spoke in her ear and told her to repeat the prayers, but she heard nothing.

She received the blessing of the Blessed Sacrament without being aware of it. Then it was that the cure took place. These are her words to me, describing the experience, as interpreted by Senhor Martim da Camara:

> First, I noticed a sharp pain in my neck and cried. I felt as though the bone had cracked in my spine. Then there was a sensation of heat, after which I felt normal. I was still crying, not knowing I was cured. Suddenly I felt as if I were bending forward instead of backward. This was merely a sensation, for I was still lying flat. I said to Margarida Tarouca, "If you help me, I'm sure I could sit up." She answered, "O, you're mad; you can't sit up." But a man, coming from the crowd, assisted me. Before, I could see only blurs of white; now I realized that I could see. In the middle of the top step of the basilica I saw a cloud of

> smoke which seemed like the smoke that comes from the chimney of a locomotive. And then I saw, at the Epistle side of the basilica, the platform and statue of our Lady which were really there.

Dona Margarida did not realize what had taken place, and when she saw Natalia sitting up, she scolded her: "You are sick. Lie down, girl; this will do you harm!" Natalia answered, "I will not lie down; I'm tired of bed." Dona Margarida then asked her how she felt. Natalia answered that she felt no more pain. Dona Margarida asked her if she thought she could stand. Natalia said she was not sure but offered to try.

With assistance, Natalia rose and stood, supporting herself on the handles of her stretcher. She became dizzy and felt weak and had to rest her head on Dona Margarida's shoulder. She was still so dazed that she did not realize what had taken place. When she was asked to walk, she was told that they were taking her to the hospital. Natalia cried and protested, "But I want to go to Fatima!" Dona Maria and another servita, Senhora Dona Maria Amelia Franqueira, assisted her as she walked in the procession in front of the statue of our Lady.

Natalia said that the walk back to the hospital was very painful, that she felt as if her ankles were breaking. Her arms were now relaxed and movable but she sensed in them a weight and weakness. When she arrived at the foot of the long steps that go up to the hospital, her servitas released their support and had her try going up alone but remained close to help her if necessary. Leaning against the wall she succeeded in getting to the top and entered the chapel.

The crowd had hailed her cure during the procession from the steps of the basilica and had thronged about her, throwing flowers and crying out, "Miracle, miracle!" Nurses had protected her from them by making a ring about her. Now, in the chapel of the hospital she was unable to say as much as a Hail Mary before the excited crowd stormed in to see her. Again the nurses had to shield her and hurry her off to the infirmary.

The doctors examined her and found that all infection had disappeared from her head and that the wounds on the side of her head and in back of her ear had closed.

Natalia said that she sat on the same bed where the night before she had suffered so much pain. Someone brought her a bowl of chicken soup, the only food that she had at Fatima. Recounting this detail of the story to me, Natalia laughed and declared, "Nothing ever tasted so good!"

To get her safely from the hospital without attracting the attention of the crowd, her friends had her change from the shroud she was wearing to the uniform of a servita, and then hurried her to a waiting bus. The bus took them to Chão de Maçãs. In alighting from the bus Natalia bumped her head on the doorway. Everyone was worried, but she suffered no harm. She slept comfortably on the train all the way down to Lisbon.

On the following day, May 14, Dona Maria Mascarenhas and her sister accompanied Natalia to the São José hospital to see Dr. Mendonça to have him certify the cure. They brought with them a letter from Dr. Pereira Gens, written at Fatima, requesting that Dr. Mendonça make out a declaration of her condition on her departure from the São José hospital and the condition in which he now found her.

Dr. Mendonça was surprised to hear that Natalia was there. He assumed that she was on a stretcher and went looking for her in the emergency room. Natalia saw him but did not know that he was looking for her.

"Where is she?" he demanded of a nurse. "I have looked and can't find her."

"Natalia is not on a stretcher; she is up," the nurse answered.

"Call her," said Dr. Mendonça.

Natalia came to the door of the waiting room. Dr. Mendonça looked greatly surprised. He turned to the ladies who were with her and declared, "We could never have put her in this state!"

When another doctor who had not treated her but knew her case came along, Dr. Mendonça stopped him and asked, "Do you know her?"

"It is Natalia," the doctor said.

"Do you remember her, how she was?" Mendonça asked.

"I remember."

"Do you see the difference?"

"It is fantastic; it is curious!" said the other.

Dr. Mendonça made her sit down and examined her head. He found the wounds closed. "This was flowing a very short time ago," he said.

Natalia replied, "It was flowing until the thirteenth."

The doctor then removed the dressings from her ear. They came out, according to Natalia, "as clean as if they had not been put there." Then the doctor washed her ear and touched it with a probe. This made the blood flow. He put in more dressing and asked her to return the following day. He commanded Natalia to bend and to sit down and to perform several other exercises to satisfy himself that she had regained freedom of muscular activity. He then asked the ladies with her to write an account of Natalia's trip to Fatima.

On the next day, Natalia returned. Dr. Mendonça removed from her ear a perfectly clean dressing. Still he insisted on prolonging the experiment and kept her returning day after day for new examinations and for the renewals of dressings. The dressings always came out unstained.

Meantime, Dona Maria was growing impatient of Dr. Mendonça's hesitancy to declare his opinion of the cure to the press. On May 27 she asked what he was going to do about the papers. He stated that he had given a release to the press. "Do you think the cure is extraordinary?" Dona Maria asked.[4]

"It may not be for others, but it is for me," the doctor said. Then he went on, "We could not have made her as she is now. For me it is as if I had cut off her arm, put it on the top of this desk, and sent her off to Fatima without an arm and she returned with two arms without anyone having touched her and without any defect, and I still saw the arm that I had cut off, on top of the desk."

Natalia turned her head and lifted the hair in back of her ear to show us the scar where the mastoid wound had been; then she parted the hair on the side of her head to show the location of the other wound.

Natalia said that she was now a nurse at the Santa Casa de Misericordia in Lisbon. She told us that she took up nursing with the motive of working to remedy the state of irreligion that she had found among so many nurses during her illness.

She is also a servita now at Fatima. Because she cannot afford to make all six trips of the major pilgrimages each year, the

[4] Miss Christina Casademont of Lisbon interviewed Dr. Mendonça at my request in May and June 1948. She read the manuscript of this chapter to him. Then, after reviewing the hospital file of the case, Dr. Mendonça on June 10, 1948, wrote for me his verification of Natalia's cure. Miss Casademont obtained also signed statements of their having witnessed the miracle from Dona Maria and Dona Margarida.

bishop has dispensed her so that she may retain the privilege with attendance at only the May and October pilgrimages.

I asked her how many miracles she had seen at Fatima in the ten years she had served there. She replied, "I have seen so many miracles, I can't say how many." I insisted on some approximation of a figure: "By 'so many' do you mean tens or hundreds?" She said, "Perhaps more than a hundred."

At the conclusion of our visit Natalia showed us a little Fatima shrine in the next room, with a small statue of our Lady on a corner bracket decorated with flowers.

At my request she promised to bring me photographs of herself taken at Fatima after the miracle. She volunteered to bring also a copy of the book that she had shown us at the beginning of the interview.

I asked her to make a statement in my notebook. She wrote the following:

> I declare that it was with pleasure that I partially explained my cure at Fatima on the thirteenth of May, 1937, a miracle that became widely known to the glory of the Most Holy Virgin.
>
> I set my hand,
> *(Signed)* Natalia Maria dos Santos
> 24-2-47

16

THE DOVES OF BOMBARRAL

Commonly shared experiences of extraordinary proportions are always popular topics of conversation. They are generally of the calamitous or, at least, notably disturbing variety—floods, quakes, tornadoes, or something like the great snow of 1947 in New York. People in Portugal talk of the doves as of a common, national experience of startling magnitude; only the incident of the doves was one of common delight rather than disturbance. It took place in December 1946, just two months before my stay in Portugal.

A notice of the happening had appeared in a copy of *A Voz de Fatima* that I had seen before I left the United States, but it was not sufficiently explained to appear exactly wonderful. On the first day of my visit in Lisbon, the Dominicans told me more of the story, and then the Wainewrights and the Stilwells. Thereafter I heard something of the doves from nearly everyone

I met. Mother Corte Real at Sardão supplied details of the beginning of the story and gave me several prints of a photo taken of the doves among the flowers beneath the statue during the celebration. The cardinal spoke of them to me and remarked that they had already become decorative motifs in new statues of Our Lady of Fatima.

The word *miracle* is seldom used about the doves. The fact of miracle seems either to be regarded as obvious in the character of the incident or simply left to the judgment of the auditor. The accent of the story is rather that of the completely charming addition that the presence of three doves made for over a week to the homage paid to the Queen and Patroness of Portugal.

The year 1946 was one of celebration in Portugal, civil and religious, because it was the third centenary of the reign of the Blessed Virgin over the country. In 1646 King João IV, at Vila Viçosa, before the Cortes Gerais had lifted the crown from his head, placed it at the feet of a statue of the Blessed Virgin, and declared her to be the Queen and Patroness of Portugal under the title of the Immaculate Conception. Then by oath he had bound himself and his successors to defend the dogma that the Blessed Virgin was conceived free of original sin. By order of the king the event was inscribed on stone tablets in every town and city of the land. Portugal became A *Terra de Nossa Senhora*. Thereafter the monarchs of Portugal never wore the crown, because it was regarded as belonging properly only to our Lady.

There were two high points in the celebration of this third centenary. On May 13, 1946, before seven hundred thousand pilgrims gathered at the Cova da Iria, His Eminence Benedetto Cardinal Masella, as personal legate of His Holiness, Pope Pius XII, placed a precious crown on the head of the little statue of Our Lady of Fatima. The jewels of this crown were donated by the women of Portugal. Thus papal action had further recognized the providential role of the Blessed Virgin in the history of Portugal. Our Lady of the Immaculate Conception renewed and continued her rule over Portugal with the additional title of Our Lady of Fatima.

For December 8, the feast of the Immaculate Conception, a great celebration was planned. The statue would be brought from Fatima to Lisbon in a solemn procession and before it, in the name of the hierarchy, the government of the republic, and the people of Portugal, the cardinal patriarch of Lisbon would renew the consecration of the nation to the Immaculate Conception in Lisbon's ancient cathedral, the *Sé Velha.*

The procession started out from Fatima on November 22. The statue rode on a platform about twelve feet long and six feet wide that built up in steps to a height of about four feet. Covered with white flowers, the platform was carried by men amid excited demonstrations of homage, welcome, and *saudades*, from town to town along the ninety-mile route from Fatima to the capital. At every town there were formal reception ceremonies performed by civil officials and religious services conducted by the clergy. The statue was venerated in all-night vigils in churches along the route; then, after Mass each morning, the journey was resumed.

The doves entered the procession at Bombarral, a city about forty miles out of Lisbon.

Dona Maria Emilia Martins Coimbra, a resident of Bombarral, had planned a very special personal act of devotion to our Lady. She had intended to have a triumphal arch built with a floral crown at its top in which there would be concealed six white doves. A cord would be drawn releasing the doves, and there would be a beautiful flutter of white wings as the statue passed under the arch.

Dona Maria wrote to a friend in Lisbon named Dona Candida Ponces de Carvalho, of Rua Braamcamp 84, asking her to purchase the doves. On November 28 Dona Candida bought six white doves from a vendor at the market in the Praça da Figueira at the cost of seventy-eight escudos and sent them on November 29 to Dona Maria.

One of the doves died on the way.

The arch could not be constructed before the procession reached Bombarral on December 1. In place of her original plan, Dona Maria had two little girls go out before the statue and set the doves free. Two doves flew away. The other three flew to the statue and settled in the flowers at its feet.

At first, the men carrying the statue regarded this as a nuisance; they feared that the doves might soil the statue, and they tried to shoo them away. But the doves would not leave. When they were flushed from their positions, they only fluttered about and returned. Their persistence finally impressed the crowd, and they were permitted to remain.

The journey from Bombarral to Lisbon took five days. During nearly all of this time the doves remained calmly at the foot of the statue, nestling in the flowers on the platform or simply sitting quite still on, or in front of, the plinth, or base, of the image. They flew off only occasionally and briefly in search of food, then returned to their chosen position.

In his Christmas sermon Cardinal Cerejeira spoke at length of the doves and enumerated the circumstances that gave remarkable emphasis to their continued presence on the platform of our Lady's statue: "At times they took flight briefly, but they were so attached to their place that neither the clamor of the multitude, nor the sound of music, nor the explosion of firecrackers, nor rain, nor wind, nor cold, nor day, nor night, nor the falling of flower petals and branches—nothing could make them depart." He might have added the disturbance of an airplane that swooped down close to the statue from time to time on the way from Loures to Lisbon to shower it with flowers.

The doves performed the first of several strange maneuvers when the statue arrived at the Church of Our Lady of Fatima, a new parochial church in Lisbon. The cardinal met the procession at the church door and delivered an address welcoming the Queen of Portugal to the capital. The doves left the statue, went over to where the cardinal was speaking and looked at him as if they were listening to and understanding what he was saying.

The statue remained for two days in this Church of Our Lady of Fatima. Inside the church the doves seemed to feel free. They flew about between the platform and the patriarchal throne, although most of the time they were seen in their accustomed place.

On December 7, during the lengthy distribution of Holy Communion, one of the doves perched with wings open on top of the crown on the head of the statue. The other two flew to the top of the ceiling and hid themselves, "as though," the cardinal said, "their mission had already been accomplished."

The great procession through the streets of Lisbon from the Church of Our Lady of Fatima to the *Sé Velha* began at about ten o'clock in the evening, on December 7. This is Cardinal Cerejeira's description of the behavior of the doves at the point of departure: "When the image of our Lady was about to leave the Church of Our Lady of Fatima on its way to the *Sé* [cathedral], in the most glorious acclamation ever given to a queen of Portugal, we saw two little doves that, since Bombarral, nothing could move from the image, poised on the edge of a stained-glass window—that of the angels in glory, which surrounds the

Throne of Exposition—closely joined together, immobile, and turned toward the image, as if saying farewell to the image and to their faithful companion at its feet."

It had been raining heavily before the departure of the statue. When the statue emerged from the church, the rain stopped suddenly, the clouds rolled back, and the moon appeared.

The route from the Church of Our Lady of Fatima to the cathedral was over three miles long. Half a million people lined the sidewalks, and many thousands more looked on from windows along the way. The city wore festive attire. Brightly colored draperies hung from balconies and windows. There was an almost ceaseless shower of flower petals from the buildings. People shouted in tremendous chorus, "Hosannah to the Queen of Portugal!" and "Ave, ave Maria!" Floodlights brightened the buildings and the procession; candles were carried by the marchers and held in windows; fireworks were set off.

I did not hear or read of the actual departure of the two doves from the Church of Our Lady of Fatima, but according to the Dominican Fathers of Corpo Santo, all of whom were in the procession, the doves did rejoin their companion at the foot of the statue, for all three were with the statue and never moved from it throughout the entire march from the church to the cathedral.

Mr. Guy Wainewright wrote of the doves in a letter soon after the event, part of which describes the arrival of the statue at the cathedral:

> On the Saturday evening the statue was borne in a candlelight procession of hundreds of thousands of people—with trumpeters on horse, and the cardinal and bishops in their robes, and members of religious orders—through

> the thronged streets of Lisbon to the beautifully floodlit cathedral, which we see well from our windows.
>
> I went about 9:30 in the evening to take up a position by the cathedral and in front of the little church that marks the spot where St. Anthony was born. I waited there with the gradually increasing crowds. Candles were appearing in the windows. At about 1:00 a.m., when the procession arrived, I had a splendid view as they entered the cathedral. It rained a little from time to time, and the powerful searchlights, concentrated on the cathedral, produced at one time a rainbow—which often seems to go with Our Lady of Fatima. There were some trees and grass where I stood by the pavement, and the moon was out over the cathedral.
>
> As our Lady was taken into the cathedral, amid the singing of the seminarists and others, one of the doves—they had never left her—flew up onto a topmost pinnacle of the cathedral and was still perched there when I left about a quarter to two.

A report had been circulated that the doves were tied to the flowers. Father Gardiner wished to satisfy himself on this point. Inside the cathedral, he told me, he left the line of march, went over to the platform, and slapped his hand down between the two remaining doves that were sitting among the flowers. They were startled and flew up for a moment—no strings attached to them—then went back to their place.

There was a night-long vigil in the cathedral. In the morning on the feast of the Immaculate Conception, December 8, the cardinal celebrated Pontifical Mass. In the afternoon there was a solemn Te Deum at which all the hierarchy of Portugal, the president and premier of the republic and members of the diplomatic corps assisted. Following the Te Deum the centenary celebration reached its climax in the renewal of the act of consecration of Portugal to the Immaculate Conception.

At six o'clock that evening the statue was carried from the cathedral to the Praça de Comércio, or Black Horse Square, as it is commonly called, where a hundred thousand people had gathered to bid it farewell before it was placed on a fishing boat to be taken across the Tagus on its way back to Fatima.

One dove only was reported as having been with the statue on its exit from the cathedral. According to one account there was one dove still with the statue on the boat. However, Francis Stilwell, who was on board the boat at the time, stated that he did not see any dove with the statue on board. He did admit the possibility, though, that the dove or doves might have gone unnoticed in the flowers.

I have not seen or heard much reported of the doves on the return trip to Fatima. One was seen and photographed in the town of Setúbal, through which the statue passed on December 13. Doves were mentioned in a press report as being with the statue in the town of Entrocamento on December 22.

The procession reached Fatima on Christmas Eve.

There are two doves, which I saw at Fatima, now kept in a cote beneath the eaves of the Chapel of the Apparitions. Some say that they are two of the three doves of Bombarral; others that they flew into the Sanctuary upon the return of the statue. The important part of the story is that of the presence and conduct of the doves through the week of December 1 to December 8. Yet one or more of them may have accompanied the statue for over three weeks.

The cardinal and others pointed out several appropriate symbolic features about the doves: the dove of Noah's ark is the symbol of peace; the Holy Spirit was represented in the image of a dove at the baptism of our Lord; in the Canticle of Canticles, the soul in love with God is spoken of in the figure of a dove; the Christian soul was symbolized by a dove in the catacombs; our Lord used the dove as a symbol of the virtues of innocence, meekness, and simplicity in the Gospels. The number three could stand for the Persons of the Blessed Trinity, the theological virtues, the three children to whom our Lady appeared at Fatima, or the three centuries of Portugal's consecration to the Immaculate Conception, which the doves helped to celebrate.

Irmã Dores referred to the doves in a letter answering an inquiry I had made about the positions of the children during the apparitions. She told me that she did not remember the locations of the children, or whether they were standing or kneeling, or had their hands folded, and so forth. Then, in evident protest against my intention of making statues of the children, she wrote, "Instead of the statues of the three children, it would not be bad merely to symbolize them with the three little doves at the feet of our Lady."

Whatever fitness there may be symbolically to the presence of the doves, it seems that the very fact of their presence is adequate reason for wonder. One may reasonably ask for more scientific information about doves in general and these three doves in particular than I am able to give before feeling compelled to admit that the doves of Bombarral are an addition to the miraculous evidences of Fatima. But to be quite sure that they are not, one would have several noteworthy problems to solve!

Why, for instance, did two fly away and three remain? What attracted the three to stay despite rain, cold, noise—especially the startling noise of firecrackers—and brilliant illumination? Why did they never take other positions for five days until exactly at the moment when the cardinal greeted the statue? What suddenly loosed their wings inside the Church of Our Lady of Fatima? What inspired one of them to stand on top of our Lady's crown with wings extended during Holy Communion? Why did two pose side by side so fixedly on the windowsill inside the church while the statue was leaving? What fixed them again at the foot of the statue for three hours during the tumultuous procession through the streets of Lisbon to the cathedral? Why were they always in front of the statue, always at its feet? Why did one of them punctuate the termination of the journey by picking the cathedral of all the hundreds of buildings along the way for its dramatic flight to the top of the tower?

If all this adds up to a fairly reasonable argument for a supernatural explanation, then it can be said that with the doves of Bombarral God has rounded out the miraculous testimonies to the message of Our Lady of Fatima through every order of creation. In a preparatory way, angelic nature testified at the Cabeço in the appearances of an angel to the children in 1916; human nature has given witness in the numerous miraculous cures at the Cova; plant life provided evidence in 1917 in the movement of the azinheira tree during the June apparition and in the fragrance of the branch that Jacinta brought to her aunt from the August apparition; mineral creation gave the promised proof of Fatima's truth in the miracle of the sun on October 13, 1917. Now the animal kingdom has proclaimed the truth of Fatima through the doves of Bombarral.

Those who doubt that the performance of the doves was a miracle will admit, I trust, that it was extraordinary and that Dona Maria Emilia Martins Coimbra of Bombarral got much more than she expected for her seventy-eight escudos.

17

THE MIRACLE OF THE SUN

The best reason for believing in Fatima is the one that the Blessed Virgin herself gave in the beginning, the miracle of the sun, on October 13, 1917. About seventy thousand people saw it, and all of them had gone to the Cova because Lucy had said there would be a miracle at noon on that day. The prophecy had been talked about so much that even the anticlerical press had to be represented. The miracle had been foretold by Lucy as the proof that the Blessed Virgin was going to give of the reality of her apparitions.

I had hoped that in my short stay in Portugal I might meet some of the people who saw that miracle. Lucy's sisters gave me their accounts on the first day of my visit to Fatima. Now, back in Lisbon, and with only a short time remaining before I had to go on to Rome, I chanced to meet another witness, Senhora Dona Ermelinda Maria Saraiva C. Alves.

In a reading room of the hotel, Senhora Alves was visiting two Spanish ladies who were guests there. I overheard her telling her friends the story of the doves, trying to describe how beautiful the doves were. I felt that they would enjoy having photographs of them, so I brought prints I had from my room and gave each of the ladies one of them. In the ensuing conversation Senhora Alves added a pleasing observation to the story of the doves. She said that she had seen one of the doves, with its neck beautifully arched, drinking rainwater which was running off the edge of our Lady's mantle. Senhora Alves later casually mentioned that she was present at the miracle of the sun in 1917.

I asked Senhora Alves many questions about the miracle. Her account was very much like those of Maria and Teresa. One point that had puzzled me in descriptions I had read was the way in which the sun seemed to move. It is usually spoken of as spinning around.

Making use of an ash tray to represent the sun, I moved it in two ways on a table—first, by holding it firmly and describing a circle on the table top; then, by turning it in one spot. I asked her which of these movements the spinning of the sun resembled. She said the second. The sun appeared to spin around on its axis and to come toward the earth. She declared also that it seemed to increase in size visually, as does any approaching object.

I asked Senhora Alves if she would kindly write out her testimony for me. She said that she would and she brought the following account to the hotel a few days later:

> I was one among the thousands of persons who assisted at the phenomenon at Fatima on the thirteenth day of

October of 1917, about a year before the end of the Great War. The description of this extraordinary phenomenon is well enough known, varying little from testimony to testimony in words. It is always the same in principle and may be summed up as follows.

Weeks before, Lucy, the visionary of Fatima, had pronounced an extraordinary fact, so that we were not surprised by what we saw.

At noon of that day the visionary exclaimed to the multitude that had gathered around, "Look at the sun!" At the time it had been raining torrentially.

Suddenly the clouds broke apart, rushing dizzily to the sides, and the sun appeared shining in the sky, showing itself like a silver phosphorescent disc, turning on itself and taking on successively (and not simultaneously) different colors: red, white, blue, and orange.

All of this was seen distinctly without the vision being blinding, despite the fact that it was midday and the sky around the sun was completely clear of clouds.

Then the sun appeared to detach itself from the sky and to come toward the earth. The multitude fell on its knees, weeping.

The sun returned to its normal position after this truly fantastic dance, and one could no longer stare at it.

All of this passed in a few seconds.

It was thus that I witnessed the sun on the thirteenth day of October of 1917, as did also thousands of persons of all social positions.

If that phenomenon had not been of supernatural origin, Fatima would not have thrived these thirty years as it still does.

The supernaturality of Fatima has, fortunately, preserved Portugal from war without the slightest harm.

(Signed) Ermelinda Maria Saraiva C. Alves.
Lisbon, 22nd of February, 1947

Senhor Carlos de Azevedo Mendes is spoken of in most of the accounts of the miracle of the sun, either by name or simply as the man who, after the miracle, lifted Lucy up over the crowd to have her tell the people what the Blessed Virgin had said. I learned that he was president of the municipality of Torres Novas. I hoped to see him on the trip that took me there for the visit with his brother, Dr. Mendes, the medical witness of the cure of Maria da Silva. Dr. Mendes told me, however, that his brother was in Lisbon at the time as a member of Parliament. He gave me his telephone number. I had Senhor Camara call Senhor Mendes and ask him if I could see him. Senhor Mendes offered to come to my hotel. He came on the evening of February 26, 1947.

Senhor Mendes was an enormous man with a large mustache, huge hands, and a booming voice. His narration and description were illustrated with forceful yet graceful gestures and were emphasized with well modulated vocal accents. The story of his association with Fatima before the days of the miracle provides a most interesting background for his testimony.

Senhor Mendes first heard of the alleged apparitions from women who came down from the Serra d'Aire to Torres Novas to sell charcoal. They said that shepherds had claimed a lady had appeared to them. With a companion Mendes rode horseback to Fatima to look into the foundations of the rumor.

Men on horseback were not a welcome sight to the people of Aljustrel and Fatima. It was less than a month since the children had been returned from their imprisonment in Vila Nova d'Ourem and the people had been severely annoyed by official threats and reprimands. Mendes and his friend were taken for soldiers or police; people turned their backs on them and refused to speak.

The adventurers then sought out the parish priest and had him intercede for them. He explained to the parents of the children that Mendes and his friend were on a peaceful mission and were not soldiers. The parents then were willing to talk. Senhor Mendes said that they "spoke in the diminutive" about the happenings at the Cova.

One after another the children were brought to him for questioning. He interviewed them singly and became deeply impressed with their candor and with the consistency of their accounts. He and his friend became convinced of the truth of the apparitions. They went with the children, then, to the Cova and said the Rosary at the tree of the apparitions. Lucy led the Rosary and the others followed.

"There was something about the way that Lucy prayed that deeply impressed me," Senhor Mendes said, "and I was able to pray with unaccustomed recollection and not the slightest distraction."

Back in Torres Novas, Mendes was an ardent promoter of Fatima. He wrote to his fiancée at length describing his interviews with the children and stating his conviction of the reality of our Lady's apparitions. He told me that his letter was used in the process of examination that preceded the declaration by the bishop of Leiria of Fatima's credibility in 1930.

On the thirteenth of September Senhor Mendes returned to Fatima to be present during the apparition. He had a place very near to the children during the time that they were in ecstasy.

I interrupted his story to ask if he had observed any of the extraordinary phenomena that had been reported. He replied, "People said they saw luminous rays and a silver shower, but I confess that I saw nothing."

"Do you think those people were suffering hallucinations?" I asked.

"No," he answered, "they were absolutely trustworthy; they did see."

Senhor Mendes resumed the narration. He said that after the apparition terminated, people crowded about the children to ask what had happened. He then started to lift Lucy up so that she could speak to the crowd. Before he could raise her as high as his shoulder, Lucy protested and cried out in accents of annoyance. Senhor Mendes gave an amusing imitation of Lucy's facial and vocal expressions, then declared, "She behaved in a stupid manner, saying, 'Let me alone, let me alone!'" Because of Lucy's petulance he dropped both Lucy and all the faith he had acquired in her and in the Fatima apparitions. He went back to Torres Novas a disappointed man, convinced that the children were victims of a pitiful illusion.

When October 13 came Mendes was unmoved by the general excitement that Lucy's prophecy of a miracle had aroused. His brother, home on furlough from the French front, heard of the promised miracle and wanted to go to Fatima. Carlos tried to discourage him. He told him what he had already seen and assured him that the same things would be repeated. "You don't want to go," he said. "It's not worthwhile." He argued that his brother should give his attention to his girlfriend rather than to the foolishness of Fatima. However, the brother had promised to go up to the mountain with friends and had to keep his promise. Carlos relented, "I will go up if you insist, but I will stay in the car."

Carlos's intention of remaining in the car did not work out. "I cannot explain even today," he said. "In spite of everything I was beside the children at the time of the apparition."

According to Senhor Mendes, soon after Lucy announced the coming of the Lady, she said, "Look at the sun, for the Lady is going to manifest herself!"

Senhor Mendes described the miracle in these words: "The rain stopped; the clouds split up into tatters—thin, transparent strips. The sun was seen as a crown of fire, empty in the middle. It went around on itself and moved across the sky. It could be seen behind the clouds and in between them, rolling around and moving horizontally. Some cried, 'I believe!'; others, 'Forgive!' The crowd prayed in terror."

Senhor Mendes commented that the miracle had the effect of making his hair stand on end.

I asked him about the colored lights mentioned to me by all the others and reported in all published accounts. He said that he did not see this color display, but that others described it to him and described also the shower of flowers.

Senhor Mendes's assertion that the sun appeared to be a ring of fire, empty in the middle, which moved horizontally across the sky behind the clouds was at variance with the other testimonies that it seemed to be a luminous disc that was visible in the blue sky and fell toward earth vertically. He seemed to be so sure of the objectivity of what he had seen that when I raised the problem of the opposite testimony he was quite certain that the others were in error. "Some were looking so fixedly at the sun," Senhor Mendes said, "that they did not observe the clouds. I insist that there were clouds in front of the sun."

It is interesting that the testimony of the unbeliever Avelino d'Almeida, reporting in the Lisbon daily O *Século* on October

15, 1917, is in agreement on these points with the descriptions given by Senhora Alves and Lucy's sisters.

I asked Senhor Mendes about the duration of the miracle. He said that it seemed to him to have been rapid, but he could not say whether it was a few seconds or a few minutes. "One was under such an impression that one could not estimate time," he added.

"Did you observe your clothes drying rapidly?" I asked.

"Everyone got a good soaking," he replied. "I did not notice whether I was wet or not. No one caught cold or became ill." He reported that when he arrived home—which, of course, was at Torres Novas, twenty miles away—his clothes were no longer wet; but the other events were so exciting, he stated, that no one thought much of this detail.

At the end of the interview I asked for the usual declaration for my notebook. Instead of a very brief statement Senhor Mendes wrote the following summary of the entire episode:

> I was in Fatima the first time on the first Friday of September, 1917. I spoke separately with the three seers. Their statements made me enthusiastic and gave me a clear impression of the supernatural.
>
> I returned on the thirteenth of September. Many people guaranteed having seen extraordinary things. I did not see anything. When the vision had ended I raised Lucy to my shoulders. To questions that were asked her she answered, crying, "Let me down!" I was shocked at the way that Lucy reacted, and I was left, as it were, with the impression that it was all a hallucination and not a vision. I lost heart with this attitude and thought of not returning again to Fatima.

But on the thirteenth of October, at the request of a member of my family, I did return to Fatima after all, declaring, however, that I would not leave the roadway. But then, without knowing how, I again found myself next to the seers at the spot of the apparitions.

At a given moment, Lucy called out to us, "Look at the sun, for the Lady is going to manifest herself." Exactly at this moment, the clouds parted, taking on the appearance of tatters, and behind them the sun, like a crown of fire, was moving, turning on itself. The impression this caused on the thousands of spectators was one of utter awe and emotion.

After this I again raised Lucy to my shoulders and then onto a rock. Then, in perfect contrast with the attitude of the thirteenth of September, she spoke to the people as if she were preaching: "Do penance! Our Lady wants you to do penance." This change of attitude impressed me, for this was the message of Fatima that she was preaching to the world.

(Signed) Carlos Mendes,
Lisbon, the 26th of February, 1947

The testimony of Senhor Mendes is the fourth eyewitness account of the miracle of the sun that we have seen. These testimonies supply us with sufficient information for certain interesting observations. There is common agreement on some points and, on others, definite disagreement.

First, there can be no doubt that the crowd was generally aware of the promise of a miracle. That is why there was such a crowd. Before Lucy spoke, there was no suspicion of the nature of the miracle to be expected. Lucy herself had no idea. The torrential rain would certainly not have predisposed people to expect a solar phenomenon. Accounts of the miracle itself agree in certain basic respects, which are, after all, the most important: the rain stopped, and the clouds parted suddenly when Lucy spoke; something most extraordinary seemed to happen to the sun; whatever the character of this happening, the effect on the crowd was terrifying and inspired open avowals of faith and repentance.

What about possible natural explanations?

I have not read of any scientific attempt to explain the miracle in terms of natural causes. Even the possibility of mass hallucination seems to have been raised only by the church authorities in their investigations and not by any opponent of the miracle. Evidence that disposed of that possibility very well was forthcoming and can be found in the histories of Fatima. People in distant towns who were not thinking of the promised miracle at the time testified that they saw the phenomena of the sun falling and the lights changing.

That leaves only the possibility of everyone having seen a peculiar natural phenomenon, still unexplained. Someone suggested to me, for instance, the possibility of an "electronic storm," whatever that may be. But the solution of a natural phenomenon that everyone saw cannot survive the important differences in the accounts. Certain minor differences are, admittedly, to be expected in several descriptions of any exciting event; but some of the differences we have seen can hardly be called minor.

Senhor Mendes said that the sun was behind the clouds; the others said it was visible in the blue sky. For him the sun was a ring, or crown of fire; for the others, a solid ball or disc. Everyone else seems to have seen the sun fall toward the earth; Senhor Mendes said it went across the sky, horizontally. All but Mendes saw the colored lights. Published accounts cite witnesses who say that the sun appeared to spin around three times before it fell; the four who gave me their testimonies described the movement of the sun as a single, continuous action. The three who saw the sun fall said it fell in a straight line; some published accounts speak of it falling in a zigzag path. Estimates of the duration of the miracle vary from a definite statement in some reports of twelve minutes to the "few seconds" of Senhora Alves's account. But the greatest argument of all against the explanation of the miracle as a natural phenomenon is the fact that Mrs. Stilwell's aunt did not see the sun at all—in fact, saw nothing extraordinary but the sudden stopping of the rain.

But even if a natural phenomenon could be imagined as the explanation and some solution be devised for the variations in the manner in which it was perceived (and for the nonperception by Mrs. Stilwell's aunt), the problem of Lucy's prophecy would still remain. How did an unschooled peasant girl of ten discover three months in advance that on October 13, 1917, at noon, there would be an extraordinary natural phenomenon?

It seems unnecessary and, in fact, contrary to the evidence to suppose that God actually let the sun fall toward the earth. He would then have had to perform numberless miracles to withhold the devastating effect of such a fall upon the universe and to prevent its being observed anywhere but in the vicinity of the Serra d'Aire.

The alternative seems to be that God first scattered the clouds and stopped the rain and then, making use of the light of the sun, impressed each and every one who was impressed with the kind and degree of wonder suited to the needs and dispositions of each. We do not presume to know God's intention, but if He wished to forestall the interpretation that the miracle could have been a natural phenomenon He certainly did just that by varying the impressions.

The miracle of the sun combined many wonders—the prophecy of Lucy, the coincidence of the miracle with the words of Lucy, the extraordinary breaking up of the clouds and cessation of rain, and seventy thousand simultaneous wonders of perception among the people present at the Cova and scattered over the Serra for whom the sun appeared in frightening activity.

18

ADEUS, LISBOA!

At the beginning of this second visit to Lisbon I received a telegram from Vila Nova de Gaia: "Congratulations and *saudades*. [*Signed*] Corte Real and Community." Mr. Ronald Symington had brought the news of the bishop's decision to the Sisters at Sardão the day before.

I wrote to Mother Provincial to thank her for the message and to tell her again of the pleasure I had in my stay at Sardão. I wrote also to Irmã Dores, thanking her for the interest she had shown in my work and for the unexpected help that she had given me with it. Mother Corte Real answered, saying:

> It was a pleasure to know that you are going to make the statue of our Lady and that our statue (very kind of you to say so), will soon be over the doorway of the Basilica in Fatima.
>
> We were all delighted and, since Our Blessed Lady has conducted this affair, letting you overcome all the

difficulties that might naturally occur, she will certainly bring it to a most happy close.

Irmã Dores replied also, but her letter was written later and sent to the United States. She too stated her pleasure in the news about the statue.

Mother King wrote like sentiments and conveyed the *saudades* of the community, especially those of Mother Provincial, Mother Cunha-Mattos, Irmã Dores, and Irmã Assunção. Thus friendly associations with the community of Sardão, which have continued ever since, were first renewed. The good sisters have always followed developments with messages of prayerful interest and encouragement.

The new statue became the object of much attention from those whom I had met before in Lisbon and from many persons whom I was to meet during the final week of my stay in Portugal. Cardinal Cerejeira manifested lively interest in it and made many inquiries about its production. The Dominicans of Corpo Santo rejoiced with me in the good fortune that had come of my visit to Vila Nova de Gaia and Fatima. They asked both Father Gardiner and me endless questions about the contents of the interviews, and took notes of our replies. In this week there began a pattern of activity that has since grown into a habit that may continue for life: showing of the statue, followed by discussion of Irmã Dores, explanation of the details of the apparition, and, finally, interpretation of the message of Fatima.

The Stilwells saw the statue one evening at tea. I was asked afterward if I would care to join them in the Family Rosary which was said daily at that time. At the conclusion of the Rosary, Mr. William Stilwell inquired eagerly if that was the first Family Rosary said before the new statue. He was delighted to learn that it was.

When Senhora Alves brought me her written testimony on the miracle of the sun, she asked if I would mind getting the statue again to show it to Senhor Alves. Their Spanish friends were also present. Language was a problem. The only common language was French, which I could not speak at all well. I learned that Senhor Alves understood Italian, although he could not speak it. I spoke Italian, therefore, and he spoke French. At times of vocabulary difficulties I chanced a word or two in English; the ladies would sometimes forget my handicap and speak their own tongues, Portuguese and Spanish. Seated around the statue we had a conversation that was in five languages. Despite the difficulty there was a good deal of information exchanged about Fatima and the statue.

Announcement by the bishop of Leiria that he intended to have me make the statue for the basilica resulted in some publicity that required press interviews. One of those who visited me was the Lisbon representative of an American international news agency. I asked him about a problem that has puzzled many people in the United States, the silence of the American press on the subject of Fatima. He was quite surprised when I told him that I had had a librarian of one of New York's leading newspapers look up Fatima under every conceivable reference, and that he had not succeeded in finding a single mention of it from 1917 to 1947.

"Well," said the news representative, "it's not because they haven't heard of it, for I have sent them many stories."

Of course, it must be kept in mind that the miracle of the sun occurred during the First World War and that wires from Europe were then filled with war bulletins. Also, much of the present interest in Fatima derives from the publication in 1942 by Church authorities of the more interesting details of the Fatima revelations. However, the fact remains that dispatches on important

Fatima events of more than denominational interest have been available to the American press. It is news, for instance, when seven hundred thousand people gather on a lonely mountain top, no matter what the reason. An incident such as that of the doves is certainly newsworthy. And perfectly substantiated miraculous cures should definitely make good copy. All things considered, it is difficult to understand the aloofness of American newspapers from a movement that has profoundly affected an entire nation and has received considerable recognition throughout the rest of the world.

There can be no question of the importance of Fatima among the Portuguese. There are still many unbelievers in Portugal, many, no doubt, who don't like Fatima; but I think it would be hard to find anyone who does not know about Fatima. Although I had heard of the survival of unbelief in a large part of the population, the people I met seemed not only informed about Our Lady of Fatima, but very much devoted to her. Room clerks, waiters, chambermaids, and telephone operators at the hotel asked to see the statue. When they saw it, they showed not only curiosity about the work but affection for the subject that it represented.

One day a photographer came to take pictures of the statue. After much thought he decided that the best light was to be found under a skylight over the staircase and elevator shaft. He set up his tripod in a position that blocked the exit from the elevator and forced him to make lengthy readjustments whenever passengers got off. All the chambermaids of the floor had to supervise his work. Leaning on mops and brooms, they talked gaily while they watched the operations. But they glanced at times down the stairwell, ready to retreat in case the manager appeared.

This interest of the employees of the hotel accounted for a gift that I now treasure. The telephone switchboard was in the main lobby, across from the desk. One of the operators, a black girl who spoke no English, always smiled pleasantly when we exchanged *Bom dia*. One day she beckoned to me. I went over. She was holding a medal in her hand, the face of which was a beautiful miniature painting, a reproduction in excellent detail, only an inch and three quarters long, of Murillo's *Immaculate Conception*.

"Like?" she asked.

"Yes, I think it is beautiful," I replied.

"Yours!" she stated, extending her hand in a gesture of offering. The gift amazed me, and I could literally find no words to thank her. Later I got one of the Fatima rosaries for her and had Senhor Camara explain that it had been made by Irmã Dores's sister, placed on the spot where our Lady appeared, and blessed by the bishop of Leiria.

The bishop of Leiria had one of the architects of the basilica call to bring me drawings of the building that I would need for planning the large statue. Senhor Camara interpreted. The architect did not seem to grasp the fact that the reason I was to make the statue at all was that the direction of Irmã Dores had given the model a special authenticity. He began to suggest alterations and additions that would have been incompatible with the entire history of my statue. He felt that the design was too simple and needed to be "enriched"; and, for the enriching, he showed me with approval a sketch of a statue with a crown on the head and cherubs in clouds at the feet.

I had to insist that the statue I was to make could be no other than an enlargement of the one he saw. If there was to be a change it would have to come from the bishop of Leiria.

Before I could do anything about an appeal for funds in the United States for the proposed gift of the statue for the basilica of Fatima, I had to have authorization from the bishop, in writing, that would clarify the question of design and confirm my right to undertake the work. On August 6, 1947, His Excellency sent me the following letter:

> With great pleasure should I have sculpted by you and according with the indications of Sister Lucia, the large statue for the niche in the front of the Basilica.
>
> Made in marble of Carrara and offered by the American friends of Fatima, it would show through the ages, on that place of honour, their faith and love for Our Blessed Mother.
>
> With many thanks and best wishes, I remain
>
> Yours truly in J. C.,
> *(Signed)* José, Bispo de Leiria

More recently, I requested of the bishop a statement that would make the origin of the statue even more explicit. In the meantime I had sent him a copy of the five-foot enlargement of the model that I made on my return to the United States. The bishop wrote, in part, on December 29, 1947: "Very many thanks for your letter and for the offering of the beautiful maquette for the marble statue of the Basilica of Fatima, made under the supervision of Sister Lucia and faithfully executed after her description."

In reply to my inquiry about working at the Cova da Iria he said, "Of course you can work the marble here, at the Shrine, where I will receive you with great pleasure."

The problem of difference in viewpoint between the architect and myself regarding the composition of the statue was thus solved, but during the two conferences in the hotel in Lisbon there had been moments of anxiety.

Senhor Camara became very much interested in this problem and had me meet an architect friend of his to get another professional and Portuguese opinion. I had feared that perhaps a consistency of Portuguese taste might oppose the design. It was a pleasure to find Senhor Camara's friend sympathetic with and even laudatory of, the composition of the statue and of its architectonic fitness for the niche of the basilica.

The pleasure of the Portuguese in serving Our Lady of Fatima, so well typified by the willing assistance of Martim da Camara in these interviews and in the ones with Natalia dos Santos and Senhor Mendes, was further proved in a little incident that occurred after our visit with Natalia. We stopped for coffee in a small shop near her apartment. A perfectly modern and spotless interior came as a surprise, after our walk down a rather untidy street. There were two other patrons, who, judged from their appearance, must have been of very modest means. They spoke with Senhor Camara and learned of my association with Fatima. Then, when it came time for us to leave, they insisted on paying our check. After having joked with Mr. Symington on the drive from Vila Nova de Gaia to Fatima about the custom of offering food to strangers, it was now a little amusing to find myself the object of such an offer in a way that was more than a gesture of courtesy.

On the evening that Senhor Mendes came to the hotel to tell me about the sun, I had two other appointments that I thought I had arranged to avoid conflicts. Natalia was to come at six; Senhor Mendes, at seven; and an architect and a poet, friends of Senhor Camara, would arrive for dinner at eight. Senhor Mendes came at 7:30; Natalia and a friend apologized for being late and arrived at about 7:45; a few minutes later Senhor Camara's friends came in ahead of their appointment. Natalia brought the pictures of herself that I had asked for and the book she wanted me to read about the other miracle. I had to discuss the statue and aesthetics with the architect and poet, and the miracle of the sun with Senhor Mendes. The half hour that followed was quite full and not a little funny.

Natalia had inscribed the book she brought:

> Offering of a *miracolada* of Fatima, who, as a Servita, assisted at the miracle which is here related.
>
> Natalia Maria dos Santos
> Calcada de Sto. André, 40-30 Lisbon
> 24th of February, 1947

On the evening of my departure for Rome I went with Senhor Camara and his architect friend to the Ministry of Public Works to inspect a model of the proposed plan for the enlarging and beautifying of the *Santuário* of Fatima. The ministry was in one of the long, majestic, colonnaded government buildings that flank the famed Black Horse Square, or Praça do Comércio. The English name of the square is derived from the equestrian monument of Dom José I. Inside the ministry I met still another architect, who was its director, a young man of very progressive ideas. I enjoyed a preview in miniature of what may be the future appearance of Fatima's shrine.

The government of Portugal, in recognition of the national importance of Fatima, has offered, as I understand, to remodel the Cova. If the plan is realized the present fountain, the gateway and the houses along the road south of the Cova will be removed; the hollows beside the central walk will be filled; and from a beautiful gateway of pylons far south of the present site, there will be a great concrete concourse, over seventeen hundred feet long, in the form of a quadrangle, clear of all objects, except the Chapel of the Apparitions. This concourse will extend from the entrance of the Cova to the steps of the basilica. The Chapel of the Apparitions will then receive the visual emphasis that it deserves.

There was not time to see all of Lisbon's interesting sights. But in some of the excursions already related I did have many pleasant views of the city. With John Stilwell I visited the cathedral, the *Sé Velha*, and admired the solid, massive, fortlike construction of its square, twin towers, and the gothic perfection of its interior. Nearby, we saw the quaint little church of Santo António and visited the chapel in the crypt that is said to mark the place where Saint Anthony was born. Then we visited the very modern Church of Our Lady of Fatima in a residential area on the edge of the city. Except for the darkness of the interior I thought the appearance of this church was admirable, and even the sacrifice of light was compensated for by tall, narrow stained-glass windows of fine color and design that detailed various feasts and titles of our Lady. Here it was that the doves had flown about in her honor not many weeks before.

Lisbon seemed to be a city of contrasts and variety. Parts were extremely old looking and others ultramodern. There were whole neighborhoods of splendid new apartment buildings, finished in pastel shades of solid colors, blue, rose, brown, and green, and trimmed at the bases and entrances in marble finish. Hills and parks and landscaped avenues combined with busy *praças* and crowded, age-old neighborhoods to create an overall impression of unusual charm.

When I think back on Lisbon, one scene especially always comes to mind, a small park, high on a hill overlooking the harbor. I went strolling one Sunday without any special place in mind, just enjoying the exceptional sunlight of a fine day and observing my fellow strollers who seemed to be in cheerful moods. I passed a street that dipped down steeply to the waterfront. At the top an odd little cable car, painted a bright yellow, perched precariously on its hypotenuse. The operator sat on a back seat alone, lazily reading a newspaper, and seemed not to be expecting customers. The park was at the end of the next street, a small area of grass that stopped at a retaining wall. Rooftops swept down toward the "Friendly Bay" from which Lisbon gets its name. There was a monument in the middle of the park, a heroic stone figure with swirling beard and menacing eyes and fists being defied by a miniature man of bronze. Whatever the struggle was, it seemed absurd in the placid atmosphere of the park. Children were playing around the monument and others were buying sweet rolls out of a basket from an aged woman vendor. Most of the city could be seen from this point, stretching from east to west for several miles along the rich, blue Tagus. Beyond the river, with its many boats, the sun warmed the green and brown coloring of the other bank.

A dog moved on a nearby roof that jutted up only a little above the level of the park. He was beside a skylight that was covered with dark paint. It was blackout paint. Some of it had flaked away. The war for which it had been put on did not come to Portugal.

19

ROME

Pope Pius XII blessed the statue on March 4, 1947.

Postwar Rome had a very different appearance from that of the Rome I had known during my studies in sculpture from 1933 to 1935. Then, gaudy and boastful Fascist posters caught the eye on every wall; bands played; *Bersaglieri* with plumed hats were seen daily demonstrating their fitness by running in formation through the streets. People seemed prosperous, lively. There was order, of a sort, although even then there were clouds on the horizon. Now crowds moved along the *corsos*, but they walked slowly, aimlessly, stunned by the violence of the storm that had passed. The bright trimmings of Fascism were gone. Instead of *Bersaglieri*, beggars roamed the streets.

The audience with the Holy Father was arranged by the procurator general of the Dominican Order, Father Paul A. Skehan. He introduced me to the Monsignor in the Vatican who, as *maestro di camera*, arranges the papal audiences. The Monsignor examined photographs of the statue and listened to the explanation of its origin. He said that he would do the best he could, and then, with a sort of desperate shrug, pointed to a stack of applications on his desk. I was surprised, therefore, on the following day to receive the official notice that the audience would be granted a day later.

Besides the wish to have His Holiness bless the statue, I had reasons of personal devotion for anticipating the visit with the Holy Father. In 1934, accompanied by the master general of the Dominican Order, when His Holiness was Secretary of State, he had visited my studio. Later the general had sent me to the Vatican to offer Cardinal Pacelli a bronze casting of one of my works. When he was elected Pope, I made a portrait bust of His Holiness that was given to the Apostolic Delegation in Washington by the Dominicans of Chicago. On being informed of the gift the Holy Father had his secretary of state, Cardinal Maglione, send me his expressions of appreciation and his Apostolic blessing.

Father Timothy Sparks, of the Curia of the Dominican master general, accompanied me for the audience. For a while we had feared that the audience might be canceled. *L'Osservatore Romano* had published the news that the Pope had turned his ankle and that he had suspended audiences on the day for which ours was scheduled. As it turned out, only the public audiences had been called off. The private and special audiences would be held.

Our audience was special. Those who have private audiences visit the Holy Father in his study; special audiences are for individuals and single parties also, but the Holy Father leaves his study and meets the visitors in separate parlors along a hallway. While Father Sparks and I awaited the conclusion of the last private audience, the *maestro di camera* and another monsignor discussed the question of whether the Holy Father would come out or, because of his injury of the day before, receive us in his study. When the time arrived, the *maestro di camera* signaled for us to go into the papal study. Our special audience had turned out to be private.

We knelt beside the desk of His Holiness. He spoke in English. His first remark surprised me very much. He said that he remembered me and recalled his visit to my studio. Then I mentioned the other visit, at the Vatican, and reminded him that I had made his portrait, now in the Delegation in Washington. He said that he remembered both.

I asked if I might place the statue on his desk. He acceded. Then I explained that I had just come from Portugal, where I had made the statue under the direction of Lucy of Fatima. He listened attentively, looked at the work, and smiled in evident satisfaction with it. Then, solemnly and slowly he blessed the statue.

Knowing of his devotion to Our Lady of Fatima I had felt that His Holiness would appreciate gifts associated with Fatima. I offered him one of the rosaries of Aljustrel that I had placed on the column in the Chapel of the Apparitions and a small cutting from the piece of wood of the azinheira tree on which our Lady had appeared. He graciously accepted these gifts and thanked me for them.

The Holy Father then said that he would bless us, our communities, our families and dear ones, and concluded with the Sign of the Cross.

Recognition of Fatima had been manifest in many acts of the Holy Father. On October 31, 1942 he had made a radio address to the Portuguese nation, speaking in Portuguese and participating in the closing ceremonies of the silver jubilee of the Fatima apparitions. At the conclusion of his address he had made the Act of Consecration of the world to the Immaculate Heart. He had solemnly renewed this act of consecration in St. Peter's before the

College of Cardinals on December 8, 1942. In 1942, as requested by Lucy, he had extended the feast of the Immaculate Heart to the universal Church. The image of Our Lady of Fatima had been crowned by his legate on May 13, 1946, at the Cova.

I hoped that my statue might occasion another expression of the Pope's recognition of the message of Fatima. I had thought out the petition carefully and now submitted it, speaking slowly to make sure that the Holy Father understood each word: "Will Your Holiness bless all those who are working to promote the message of Fatima in the United States?"

He said that he would and made the Sign of the Cross.

At the close of the audience the Holy Father blessed the rosaries and other religious articles that I had brought from Fatima. He then gave each of us a rosary.

Father Sparks expressed sympathy over the injury that His Holiness had sustained. The Holy Father thanked him and declared that it was nothing at all.

During all this time I studied him so intently that I had no idea of what was in the room beyond the first foot of surface on his desk. He seemed thinner and considerably older than when I had last seen him, and his hair had turned almost white. But there was no change whatever in the warmth of his smile, which reflected gentleness like that of Him whose place he takes on earth.

Father Sparks had been one of the first apostles of devotion to Our Lady of Fatima in the United States. He now saw to it that no opportunity of drawing attention to Fatima in Rome by means of the statue was neglected. He arranged visits with the master general of the Dominican Order and with the Dominican communities of Santa Sabina, the Angelicum and San Clemente, and with the Irish Dominican Sisters at Villa Rosa and the Americans at the convent of the Perpetual Rosary. Among all those visited, eagerness to learn everything possible about Fatima was general. On my own, I visited the Collegium Russicum. Since Our Lady at Fatima had prophesied the conversion of Russia through its consecration to her Immaculate Heart, I wanted this image of the Immaculate Heart, now blessed by the Holy Father, to be instrumental in emphasizing her message among those who are training at the Russian College to serve the Church in Russia. I had to go unannounced, because I knew no one who could announce me.

The rector of the college, Father De Regis, who is French, received me. His strong features and long, square beard gave him the appearance of one of Michelangelo's patriarchs. I told him about the statue and said that because of the connection between Fatima and Russia I wanted to have the statue inside the Russian College.

Father De Regis evidently took my statement to mean that I wanted to make at least a gift and possibly a sale, for he explained that statues are not used in the Oriental Rite. I had to make it clear that I merely wanted to show it to him. During the explanation he was very attentive, and when I showed him the statue he seemed pleased, but he was not inspired to suggest that I show it to the others in the house. I thought I would have to pack it up and leave without seeing a single Russian.

"Do you suppose anyone else would care to look at it?" I ventured.

After deliberating for a moment, he brought me upstairs to another official of the seminary—a Russian, at last.

By ones and twos, the other priests and the seminarians gathered until there were about twenty in the room. In Italian, for an hour and a half, we discussed Fatima, particularly the phases of the revelations related to Russia.

The problem of promoting devotion to the Immaculate Heart in Russia was raised by one of the seminarians. He stated that Orientals object to the representation of the heart. I suggested that the objection might be overcome with the proper instruction, and several agreed that this was entirely feasible. Orientals are most devoted to the Blessed Virgin and have no objection to symbolism. The Immaculate Heart could be presented successfully, one of the Russians insisted, as the symbol of our Lady's maternal love for mankind.

At the end of this visit I suggested that we all say a prayer before the image. Father De Regis led the group upstairs to a small chapel.

A screen, or iconostasis, separated the sanctuary from the body of the chapel, where we gathered. One of the seminarians placed a lectern at the left side of the screen and then put a small altar bookstand upside down on the lectern, to make a flat surface with two forty-five degree angles. A beautiful yellow humeral veil was draped over this improvised pedestal, and the statue was placed on it.

In Oriental fashion we all stood for the prayers. Father De Regis came forward wearing a long, gold-colored stole that fell to the hem of his cassock. He bowed and made the Sign of the Cross in the Oriental manner, the elbow kept close to the side, and the action terminating with the hand over the heart. He intoned a chant about half the length of an Ave. The group sang in harmony a response of similar composition and length. Invocations and responses of this litany-like prayer, which is called a Molieben, went on for several minutes. The chant was melodious and stirring. At its conclusion the rector knelt, and we all followed his action. He read in Russian the act of consecration to the Immaculate Heart. Finally, all stood for the singing in Russian of the *Sub Tuum*:

> We fly to thy patronage, O Holy Mother of God. Despise not our petitions in our necessities, but deliver us from all dangers, O glorious and ever Blessed Virgin.

The papal blessing had completed the objectives with which I had left the United States. Now, however, I was returning with a new image and a new understanding of Fatima. Irmã Dores not only had corrected my ideas of the appearance of our Lady at Fatima, but she had also explained the spiritual vision of Fatima in the message of our Lady and had encouraged me to work to make that vision better known.

In the journey back, I was to see the effects of the war that our Lady prophesied, in France, Germany, and England, a war that could have been avoided if the world had heeded her wishes and warnings at Fatima.

The day I left Rome I saw for the first time actual war damage in the ruins of the hangars at the airport. The sight of twisted steel beams seemed like sacrilege in the peaceful setting of the hills under a beautiful Roman sky.

20

THE SPIRITUAL MEANING OF THINGS

Irmã Dores knew that I intended to write a book. In a letter I received from her on my return to the United States she charged me with a task that I must now try to perform. "In your writing," she said, "please stress the spiritual meaning of things, in order to raise minds that today have become so materialistic to regions of the supernatural; so that they may understand the true meaning and purpose of the coming of our Lady to earth, which is to bring souls to heaven, to draw them to God."

There is only one more incident in this story. It is told because through it I had sorrowfully and intently to search for "the spiritual meaning of things."

On my return I went to Chicago, where, at the Daprato Studios, I could have the technical assistance necessary for finishing the five-foot copy of the statue in time for a Novena at the Church of St. Vincent Ferrer in New York City. I had only a day in New York to visit with my mother.

The statue was finished in time, and I was looking forward to its unveiling as an occasion that would bring my mother much joy.

On May 7 I was called home; my mother had had a heart attack. She was dead when I arrived.

I preached at the dedication of the statue. My mother's body was in the funeral parlor across the street.

It was Mother's Day, May 11, 1947.

We have to look honestly at Fatima. It is not what we want it to be, but what God planned it to be. In the statue that I had brought to Portugal there were pleasing preconceptions of what our Lady might have looked like. They were wrong. For the conclusion of this journey and its extraordinary developments I anticipated a day of unmixed happiness. I was wrong. Many people interpret Fatima according to their tastes and prejudices. They are wrong.

"My thoughts are not your thoughts; nor your ways my ways, saith the Lord" (Isa. 55:8).

God has proved the truth of Fatima with great miracles. We must accept that truth or run the risk of neglecting grace. If we find that our habits of thinking are at odds with what God has made known at Fatima, we had better promptly revise our thinking. Nobody likes to think about hell; divine justice is a frightening attribute that we easily ignore; penance is disturbing; devotion to the Immaculate Heart may seem like an unnecessary novelty; discussion of Russia may appear imprudent; the Rosary strikes some as monotonous and the Five First Saturdays as unduly mathematical. But all these are in the message of Fatima, and we must put them in order and understand them if we want to accept what God has said to us through Fatima in the resounding voice of miracles and prophecies.

Fatima is, first of all, a dreadful warning to the world to stop sinning. The enormity of mankind's rebellion against God and God's infinite aversion for sin form the foundation of the Fatima message. Then He gives the sinner hope in the revelation that He will accept repentance made through the Immaculate Heart of Mary. Fatima manifests the most misunderstood of the divine attributes—justice and mercy.

The three children of Fatima saw hell. The vision was not for their instruction or warning, but for ours; the Blessed Virgin had assured them that they were going to be saved. The accent on hell is tremendous. It is the first part of the Secret of Fatima; it is the reason for all the rest of the revelations. Our Lady went on to tell of temporal punishments that would be visited on the world if men did not amend their lives. We have seen them come—war, famine, persecution of the Church, the destruction of many nations. From the words of our Lady we must fear even greater affliction unless there is a change in human conduct. But we definitely miss "the spiritual meaning of things" if we think that our Lady came at Fatima to tell us how to keep out of a third world war, or how to convert Russia, or how to achieve tranquillity in our earthly existence. She came to tell us how to keep out of hell!

The temporal punishments are secondary; they are punishments that strangely impress us more than hell. Yet all the bleeding, dying, and despair of a thousand wars cannot equal the disaster of a single soul being damned. And damnation is not merely a possible evil that may arrive if we do not do what Our Lady of Fatima said; it is an actuality already claiming countless souls who did not and now never can fulfill the purpose of their existence. Fatima is intended to stop this devastation. War can come or not; it is evil, in the final analysis, only in the measure that it brings about the only final evil, the loss of souls.

"You have seen hell where the souls of sinners go," the Blessed Virgin said to Lucy. This is the first point of the Fatima message. We are free, we have abused our freedom, we are in danger of failing eternally, we must repent. "Do not offend our Lord anymore; He is already much offended," our Lady said to Lucy while seventy thousand people watched the spinning and falling of the sun.

At the August apparition our Lady said: "Pray, pray very much; and make sacrifice for sinners. Many souls are lost, because there are none to make sacrifices for them." In every apparition she urged the children on to sacrifice; and for their sacrifice she presented two motives: the reparation of offenses against the divine majesty and the conversion of sinners. In the July apparition she taught a prayer that she asked to be said whenever sacrifices were offered: "O Jesus, it is for Your love, for the conversion of sinners and in reparation for the sins committed against the Immaculate Heart of Mary." The children responded with exceptional works of penance. We are urged to do penance also, to make at least the sacrifices necessary for fulfilling our duties.

If the emphasis in the Fatima message on the danger of hell and the necessity of penance is upsetting, there are a few considerations that may rectify our judgment. No one fully understands the gravity of sin because it must be measured by the holiness of God, whom sin offends. The plea of our Lady on the mountain at Fatima is not different from the dictation of our Lord on another mount: "Enter ye in at the narrow gate, for wide is the gate, and broad is the way that leadeth to destruction, and many there are who go in thereat" (Matt. 7:13). The fire of hell cannot be extinguished by our indifference to it; nor will divine justice be altered by our failure to understand it. "Hear ye, therefore, O house of Israel: is it my way that is not right, and are not rather your ways perverse?" (Ezek. 18:25). We must admit the mystery and accept the facts of divine justice and everlasting punishment. The crime of not seeking heaven is very great. It is much better to be terrified now of hell and avoid it than to ignore it now and after death discover it. "Why will you die, O house of Israel?" (Ezek. 18:31).

"To save them the Lord wishes to establish in the world devotion to my Immaculate Heart." This sums up the second part of the Secret of Fatima. The warning of hell and earthly chastisements manifests divine justice, but it is also an expression of God's mercy. Divine mercy is further manifest in the revelation of the Immaculate Heart.

Devotion to the Immaculate Heart of Mary is not new. It was practiced by our Blessed Lord. The heart of Mary was honored with His first miracle. It was the affectionate consideration of our Lady's heart for the bridal couple at Cana that inspired her to have our Lord change water into wine. The heart of Mary is the symbol of her love. Her love is without stain of any kind, without a single blemish of selfishness—immaculate.

The angel Gabriel honored the Immaculate Heart of Mary when he saluted her as "full of grace," for grace is the sharing of God's life, and the divine life in the Christian soul is active through charity, which is love.

The Immaculate Heart is the full flowering of the grace that God bestowed on His Mother in her Immaculate Conception.

We have always known that the Blessed Virgin had an intimate share in the work of redemption and that, through her, God wills that the fruits of redemption be distributed to the souls of men. We know now from Fatima that God wishes us to honor the heart of His Mother, or, let us say, to honor His Mother, our Co-Redemptrix, through the title of her love—her Immaculate Heart.

The Immaculate Heart of Mary suffered because of sin. At Fatima she showed Lucy her heart pierced all about by thorns. God has told us now, through Fatima, that we can make reparation to Him if we repair the suffering we have caused her. The heart that received the fullness of participation in the divine life, that knew the affections of a mother for Jesus Christ during the years at Nazareth, that went through the agony of seeing Him die, that honors Him in heaven more than all the rest of creation, is now gloriously proclaimed by Him through Fatima. The Lord wishes to establish in the world devotion to the Immaculate Heart of Mary. We must not discuss the timeliness or convenience of devotion to the Immaculate Heart; we must strive in humble prayer to acquire it.

This is substantially the meaning of Fatima. There are other details, indeed, but the details must not obscure the essence of Fatima's message—namely, that for our own salvation, for the conversion of sinners, for the expiation of our sins, God wants us to honor the heart of His Mother.

The other details have to do with the means of honoring the Immaculate Heart and with the divine sanctions of this devotion—the punishments that will follow if God's merciful offer is spurned and devotion to the Immaculate Heart is neglected.

The first means declared at Fatima of paying homage to the Immaculate Heart is the Rosary. It is certainly our Lady's favorite prayer. The reason is not hard to find: the soul of the Rosary is meditation on the mysteries of our Lord's Incarnation, redemptive suffering, and glorious triumph. It is her favorite prayer because it draws us to our Lord.

The devotion of the Communions of reparation of the Five First Saturdays was made known and insisted upon in three distinct apparitions to Irmã Dores. It has simplified the manner in which we can fulfill the demands of Fatima. A great promise has been made. We are assured of the help necessary for salvation if we fulfill a series of devotional acts with the intention of making reparation to God for sin through the Immaculate Heart of Mary. The request is not vague; it is definite. From this definition can be derived the comfort of reaching an assurance that we have fulfilled the call of Fatima. We are asked to receive the sacraments of Penance and Holy Communion (Penance within a week, before or after) on the first Saturday of each of five consecutive months; and, on the first Saturdays, to say the Rosary (five decades) and, apart from the Rosary, to spend fifteen minutes in meditation on one or more of the mysteries of the Rosary.

There was a great public act of homage to the Immaculate Heart demanded at Fatima—the consecration of Russia to the Immaculate Heart by all the bishops of the world. Pope Pius XII consecrated the world to the Immaculate Heart on October 31, 1942. He made descriptive mention of Russia in that consecration. We hope for the day when this consecration of Russia to the Immaculate Heart will be solemnly renewed by the Holy Father, joined on the same day by the entire Catholic world under the leadership of all the bishops of the Church. May it not be that this saving act must wait until the devotion itself has been firmly established?

Our Lady foretold at Fatima that Russia would spread her errors throughout the world and that the results would be wars and persecution of the Church. This does not mean that Russia is the enemy of peace; it means rather that Russia—unwittingly, indeed—is the instrument of divine justice. The enemy of peace is not Russia, but sin, which abounds within all borders.

Our Lady of Fatima has prophesied absolutely that Russia will one day be converted and that a period of peace will follow. There is no indication in her message that this will be achieved before another war. Fatima must not be mistaken for merely an assurance of peace. Peace will one day come; its arrival will be hastened if men repent and honor the Heart of Mary. If they do not, the world will continue to suffer the chastisements of divine justice.

But the triumph of the Immaculate Heart in your soul and mine and in the soul of the man in the delicatessen, or of the woman across the way on the streetcar, or of the child in the classroom, or of the executive at his desk, does not have to wait for the consecration of Russia; it awaits the consecration of the individual to God in penance and in reparation through the heart of Mary.

Irmã Dores was happy to assist in making an image of the Immaculate Heart because, in the June apparition, in 1917, the Blessed Virgin told her that she must remain longer on earth in order to spread devotion to the Immaculate Heart. Then our Lady said to her, "My Immaculate Heart will be your refuge and the way that will lead you to God."

That souls may be saved through the Immaculate Heart of Mary is the reason why our Lady appeared at Fatima, why Lucy is still separated from her little friends, Francis and Jacinta, why the statue was made, why the Pope blessed it, and why this story has been written.

EPILOGUE

Early in April 1948 Lucy of Fatima (Irmã Dores) entered the cloister of the Carmelite Order in Coimbra. Her name is now Sister Mary of the Immaculate Heart.

Lucy's task of communicating the Fatima message to the world must now be finished. As long as she was needed for this work, she had to belong to an active community where she could reach and be reached by the world. Her mission fulfilled, she now becomes free to retire to the contemplative life in the seclusion of the cloister.

The Blessed Virgin appeared only to Lucy under the aspects of Our Lady of Sorrows and Our Lady of Mount Carmel on October 13, 1917. Perhaps these visions pointed out for her the two phases of her religious vocation. Having been known in the Dorotheans as Irmã Dores (Sister Dolores), she has been dedicated in name and in fact to the Sorrowful and Immaculate Heart. It must have been painful for her to bear alone to an incredulous world the burden of the Fatima message and to know the vastness of human calamity that has resulted from contempt for that message.

Lucy of Fatima may not speak again to the world, but she will always speak more importantly of the world to God and our Lady from the heights of Carmel.[5]

[5] Lucy dos Santos died on February 13, 2005.—Ed.

The ROSARY SHRINE *of* SAINT JUDE
www.rosaryshrineofstjude.org

Dear Reader,

Father Thomas McGlynn, O.P., like all Dominican friars, had a special devotion to the Rosary.

In all her appearances, the Blessed Mother repeatedly emphasized the necessity of praying the Rosary daily. This message is as important now as it was a hundred years ago, when our Lady appeared at Fatima.

That is why, a few years later, the Dominican Friars in the United States established the Rosary Shrine of Saint Jude, which resides in Washington, D.C. I am proud to be the director of the Shrine.

At the Rosary Shrine, the friars pray for the intentions of its members at daily Masses, in Rosaries, and in monthly novenas.

To learn more about becoming a part of this community, visit:

www.rosaryshrineofstjude.org.

To learn more about the Dominican Friars, visit:

www.dominicanfriars.org.

Sincerely in Our Lady of Fatima,

Father Gabriel

Father Gabriel Gillen, O.P.
Director

Sophia Institute

Sophia Institute is a nonprofit institution that seeks to nurture the spiritual, moral, and cultural life of souls and to spread the Gospel of Christ in conformity with the authentic teachings of the Roman Catholic Church.

Sophia Institute Press fulfills this mission by offering translations, reprints, and new publications that afford readers a rich source of the enduring wisdom of mankind.

Sophia Institute also operates two popular online Catholic resources: CrisisMagazine.com and CatholicExchange.com.

Crisis Magazine provides insightful cultural analysis that arms readers with the arguments necessary for navigating the ideological and theological minefields of the day. *Catholic Exchange* provides world news from a Catholic perspective as well as daily devotionals and articles that will help you to grow in holiness and live a life consistent with the teachings of the Church.

In 2013, Sophia Institute launched Sophia Institute for Teachers to renew and rebuild Catholic culture through service to Catholic education. With the goal of nurturing the spiritual, moral, and cultural life of souls, and an abiding respect for the role and work of teachers, we strive to provide materials and programs that are at once enlightening to the mind and ennobling to the heart; faithful and complete, as well as useful and practical.

Sophia Institute gratefully recognizes the Solidarity Association for preserving and encouraging the growth of our apostolate over the course of many years. Without their generous and timely support, this book would not be in your hands.

www.SophiaInstitute.com
www.CatholicExchange.com
www.CrisisMagazine.com
www.SophiaInstituteforTeachers.org

Sophia Institute Press® is a registered trademark of Sophia Institute.
Sophia Institute is a tax-exempt institution as defined by the
Internal Revenue Code, Section 501(c)(3). Tax I.D. 22-2548708.